individuals, and teams achieve life-changing goals and find work/life harmony through her New Steps Life Coaching practice. Now Monica has shared these tried and proven methods in her wonderful new book, *Doubtful to Decisive: Eight Steps to Get Unstuck and Take Action*.

"Drawing on the teachings of leadership, mindfulness, and personal improvement experts such as Stephen Covey and James Clear, Monica provides her readers with the tools and strategies necessary to develop an empowered mindset in this hard-hitting yet plain-spoken book. Monica's motto of "Dream It, Plan It, Do It, Live It" is the driving principle behind her Eight-Step "Action Cycle" that guides readers from Awareness and Acceptance of a problem or challenge to Action, Completion, and Reflection. Best of all, the book is sprinkled with dozens of anecdotes from Monica's remarkable professional career and personal life that illuminate these principles in a way that is relatable and easily understood.

"If you want to gain clarity and achieve what's truly possible in your life, Monica will help you to get there!"

—Bill Purcell, President of Greater Valley Chamber of Commerce in Shelton, CT.

"*Doubtful to Decisive* is a great guide to evaluating and readying yourself to overcome obstacles in order to move forward in life. Monica offers great ways to dig in and assess your own habits and thoughts that can prevent you from shifting into gear on any issue. I could hear her voice in my head as I read it. It felt like a coaching session in print. The Eight Steps give you all the tools you need to gain insight, get over that hump, and solve any challenge you're facing."

—Jocelyn Murray, Marketing and Event Resources, LLC.

"This book is clearly written and highly relatable. Monica cleverly weaves personal stories, insights, and expertise to guide her readers through their obstacles toward accomplishing goals with greater self-awareness, compassion, and gratitude that we're not alone in our struggles. Monica gives the reader real tangible steps to making decisions and at the same time gives them an opportunity to get to know themselves better."

—Lynda Mettler, Transformational Coach at Channeling Your Wisdom Coaching.

"If you're undecided about anything, Monica Leggett's brilliant book *Doubtful to Decisive* is for you. Her Eight Steps will guide you to achieving an action-focused mindset with remarkable results. I particularly enjoyed (and learned from) Monica's willingness to share her own personal life situations where she found herself stuck, which makes her wisdom all the more relatable to the reader. Now I don't hesitate to use these helpful steps and recommend this book to my friends, family, and business associates—nor should you!"

—Martha Rhodes, Book Shepherd and Author of *3,000 Pulses Later: A Memoir of Surviving Depression Without Medication.*

"*Doubtful to Decisive: Eight Steps to Get Unstuck and Take Action* will help you get unstuck from all the beliefs, thoughts, or excuses that keep all of us stuck from time to time. At every stage of life, there is something that holds us back from being our best selves. The repeatable framework and

Praise for *Doubtful to Decisive*

"*Doubtful to Decisive,* what a great road map—to get you from stuck to unstuck with easy-to-follow directions. Monica Leggett has written the book I wish I had access to years ago. In her compelling and very easy-to-read style, she engages you from the very beginning, giving you concrete ideas and strategies to help you achieve all those goals and dreams that you used to think were out of reach."

—Linda Larsen, Hall of Fame Keynote Speaker and Author, *12 Secrets to High Self-Esteem.*

"Leggett has turned her decades-long experience as a coach into exercises that advance our thinking, powerful questions that prompt reflection, and lessons learned that move the reader into action. *Doubtful to Decisive* is like having your own professional coach."

—Margaret H. Greenberg, MAPP, PCC, co-author of *The Business of Race: How to Create and Sustain an Antiracist Workplace and Why It's Actually Good for Business,* and *Profit from the Positive: Proven Leadership Strategies to Boost Productivity and Transform Your Business.*

"Whether you're an aspiring entrepreneur, a small business owner looking to grow, or a professional that is looking to get unstuck from any issue, you'll find Monica's book a valuable resource to help you take the necessary action towards living the life you truly deserve. Many people get overwhelmed and suffer from analysis paralysis, leading to unfulfilled dreams and businesses that plateau, and find themselves giving up on their goals. What do they all have in common: they doubt their next move! Monica has put her life's work as a personal life coach into this book and I would highly recommend you add *Doubtful to Decisive: Eight Steps to Get Unstuck and Take Action* to your reading list!"

—Ramon Peralta, Founder of Peralta Design.

"Regardless of what's happened in the past, there's no need to read another self-help manual to learn what holds you back from success. Monica Leggett combines her vast coaching expertise with the best input from the top gurus in the field. No matter how stuck you might think you are, *Doubtful to Decisive* will help you discover how to overcome your doubts and shift into decisively achieving the results you once thought were impossible."

—Tanya Detrik, Ghostwriter, Speaker, and Author of *This is Grief* and *Waking Up with Nora*.

"Monica Leggett doesn't merely 'give advice,' she lives the advice (in logical, well-ordered steps) with a vulnerability and clarity that makes her such an exceptional coach. This book will take you exactly where the title promises—from doubtful to decisive, with specific exercises, stories, and explanations all along the way!"

—Randye Kaye, Voice talent, Actress, Speaker, and Author of *Happier Made Simple: Choose Your Words, Change Your Life*.

"For the past fifteen years, I have watched in awe as Monica has helped countless numbers of small business owners, exercises shared will guide your transformation to discovering your Best Self and a path to embracing and maintaining it, even as life brings us new challenges.

"The examples Monica used in the book are very relatable. I saw many parts of myself from my career and as a coach, business owner, parent, and partner in a new and different light. Monica's book gave me a deeper perspective and insight on the value of controlling the things in life we can and not only getting through the things we can't but accepting the lessons learned from them to become our best self."

—Maryann Croce, Small Biz Vantage, Business Coach.

"Monica Leggett's commitment to helping people get into action in every part of their life is present throughout this book. She has presented three of my favorite coaching programs that include a structure based on inner parts: Internal Family Systems (IFS), The Power of TED* (*The Empowerment Dynamic), and Positive Intelligence. These programs, at separate times, have helped me explore 'my parts' that either are helping or hindering me. I am eager to capitalize on the many exercises she has created in her masterpiece, *Doubtful to Decisive*."

—Tom Horne, Business Coach to family-run businesses at The Full Picture.

"If you are tired of digging the dead-end ruts in your life deeper—of trying to show up different but ending up in the same old place again—try engaging with Monica Leggett's MAP (mindset / assessing / planning), a key part of the successful change process in her new book, *Doubtful to Decisive*.

She breaks down ways to change step by step, highlighting the many places that most of us have lost our way again and again. Offering practical exercises, tips, and heartening stories, Monica provides a wealth of resources to help you chart your course and stay on track without shooting yourself in the foot...again!"

—Elizabeth A. Kaye, Leadership Coach and Consultant.

"Monica started out as my coach, then mentor, and now friend. This book is a coaching session with Monica. I hear her authentically speaking. I cannot wait to have this book as a reference for my own clients. Thank you, Monica, for breaking down the often-difficult decision-making process and giving us this tool to use."

—Renata Taylor, Renata Taylor Coaching.

"In *Doubtful to Decisive,* Monica Leggett has taken her years of coaching with hundreds of clients, studying various coaching practices, learning from leading experts, and has compiled her wisdom and insights into the *Eight Steps to Get Unstuck and Take Action.* She helps the reader move from focusing on their problems and overwhelm to focusing on the intentions and outcomes they desire and finding the motivation to move forward. Monica clearly lays out the foundation for being able to implement her Eight Steps in the first part of her book by exploring topics such as Shifts, Mindset, and Inner Work. Through personal stories, client anecdotes, and many wonderful exercises, she encourages the reader to dive deeper into the material by exploring what is keeping you stuck and how by getting in touch with your Best Self you can reach the desired outcomes you are looking for. As a coach, I am looking forward to implementing Monica's insights and techniques with my clients and with myself!"

—Ele Dootson, Certified Empowerment Coach at Radiant Light Coaching.

"After reading *Doubtful to Decisive,* I think I've gotten more done in twelve hours than in the last three months. I made several very difficult decisions, communicated as best I could, and felt such a sense of relief and accomplishment. Monica Leggett's book has CHANGED me the way very few books have. The book is helping me purge my life of things that aren't working and then add back in the parts that I miss or that were working. This is not easy! I was stuck in a couple of areas regarding time and projects, and I was able to see several things very clearly.

"Monica consistently helps the reader remember where we've been successful in the past, and by the end, I could feel a shift in my thinking. She is very vulnerable, sharing stories that make the reader feel like she is already on their team, helping them, as one of them not as a 'do this! do that!' but as 'I've been there', or even, 'I'm still there, all the time, and these tools help me.'

"The book is written in a motivating and attainable voice. Nothing feels like 'too much' and I like that she puts life preservers in there by saying, 'If this feels like too much, try using this tool to work through that.' Monica doesn't just expect us to be in Basic Training, grinding it out in the rain with the flu, hungry and tired, and 'just do it.' This is a very realistic approach and has tools built right in along the way to give this process the best chance of success.

"Just today, I was feeling overwhelmed and I said, 'What did Monica say in her book?' and then I just did the next tiny doable thing and before I knew it, I was done with the task. If you are feeling stuck or frustrated or overwhelmed, you must get *Doubtful to Decisive!*"

—Lynn S., Entrepreneur and Owner of two online businesses.

Doubtful to DECISIVE

Eight Steps to Get Unstuck and Take Action

Monica Leggett

Copyright (C) 2023 Monica Leggett. All rights reserved.

No part of this publication shall be reproduced, transmitted, or sold in whole or in part in any form without prior written consent of the author, except as provided by the United States of America copyright law. Any unauthorized usage of the text without express written permission of the publisher is a violation of the author's copyright and is illegal and punishable by law. All trademarks and registered trademarks appearing in this guide are the property of their respective owners.

For permission requests, write to the publisher, addressed "Attention: Permissions Coordinator," at the address below.

Publish Your Purpose
141 Weston Street, #155
Hartford, CT, 06141

The opinions expressed by the Author are not necessarily those held by Publish Your Purpose.

Ordering Information: Quantity sales and special discounts are available on quantity purchases by corporations, associations, and others. For details, contact the publisher at hello@publishyourpurpose.com.

Edited by: Blue Dulac, Nancy Graham-Tillman
Cover design by: Nelly Murariu
Typeset by: JetLaunch

ISBN: 9798887979953 (hardcover)
ISBN: 9798887970882 (paperback)
ISBN: 9798887970899 (ebook)

Library of Congress Control Number: 2023918564

First edition, January 2024.

The information contained within this book is strictly for informational purposes and is not offered as a substitute for direct assistance from a qualified professional. If such level of help is required, please seek out a professional provider for physical, emotional, financial, or legal support. The Author and Publisher offer no guarantees about the results of your efforts after reading this book. The author is providing information based on their training and experience. The reader's ultimate success or failure will be the result of their own efforts and persistence, as well as their circumstances. The material may include information, products, or services by third parties. As such, the Author and Publisher do not assume responsibility or liability for any third-party material or opinions. The publisher is not responsible for websites (or their content) that are not owned by the publisher. Readers are advised to do their own due diligence when it comes to making decisions. Reading this book implies your acceptance of this disclaimer.

Publish Your Purpose is a hybrid publisher of non-fiction books. Our mission is to elevate the voices often excluded from traditional publishing. We intentionally seek out authors and storytellers with diverse backgrounds, life experiences, and unique perspectives to publish books that will make an impact in the world. Do you have a book idea you would like us to consider publishing? Please visit PublishYourPurpose.com for more information.

ACKNOWLEDGMENTS

I'm filled with gratitude and appreciation for my family, friends, teachers, coaches, colleagues, and clients who have inspired and supported me on my coaching journey. This book represents thousands of hours of classes, coaching sessions, discussions, presentations, and pages read in order to become the best coach possible. I wanted to become a coach to help others and found it has transformed my life as well.

I'd like to thank my family:

My late sister Grace, who initiated my personal growth journey by inviting me to a coaching class in 2006. I desperately wish you were still here to read this. Little did we know, seventeen years ago, that you would change my life so dramatically.

My daughters Christine and Melissa, you inspire me every day with your generosity and kindness. You have always been my greatest cheerleaders and willing sounding boards.

My husband Steve, my partner in life for over forty-three years, you are the Yang to my Yin. Thanks for putting up with my many moods as I "birthed another baby" and for allowing me to share some of our stories.

My siblings Sheila, Katherine, Johnny, Grace, Patrick, Charlotte, Paul, Ilene, and Julia, you were instrumental in my nurturing and now are my friends. I've learned from each and every one of you.

My family by marriage, especially Dolores Leggett, you've been the mom I lost thirty years ago and I'm so grateful you're still in my life now.

To those who helped me find my voice:

Anna Cole, it was a fortuitous day when we ended up in the same coaching class in 2007. We became fast friends, coached each other through the certification process, and developed programs to teach others what we were learning. It was one such course that eventually led to my eight-step Action Cycle. I will be forever grateful you came into my life at just the right time.

To Sheila Schimmel, Elizabeth Kaye, Tom Horne, Ele Dootson, Lynda Mettler, and Renata Taylor; more than anything else, you listened as I shared, gave me feedback when I asked, discussed when I needed to work through my ideas, and gave continual support and encouragement. You share my passion for helping others and are ever-present with curiosity, generosity, and encouragement.

I coach in the very specific niche where business meets personal, so it is very fitting that the "business networking group" I co-created, Authentic Connections, has become a place of both business and personal growth for all of us. I thank each and every woman who has attended a meeting, presented on a topic, led a discussion, or shared their wins, thoughts, and gratitude. It has been an honor and a pleasure facilitating discussions and sharing my work over these last fourteen years. A special thanks to Megan Crandlemire and Tanya Detrik, co-facilitators and good friends. Thanks also to Ethel-Anne, Bette Lynn, Martha, Lynn, Sheila, Rosanne, Adriene, Dee, Julie, Beth, Lisa, Renata, Theresa, Nancy, Kaleigh, Marta, and Stephanie.

I want to acknowledge the many supporters of my writing journey:

Midge Noble, you've been the glue that kept me in my chair! You showed up for me twice a week for over eighteen months, and it helped me show up—for you, for myself, and for my goal of publishing a book. Having an accountability partner going through the same process has made all the difference in the world. Some people thrive on their own, but I am not one of those people. May your book, *Gay With God,* go on to help people transform pain and shame with authentic power.

I would like to thank the early readers who helped me during the editing process: Martha, Lorraine, Ele, and Renata, your support was so encouraging. To David Emerald, Donna Zajonc, and Linda Larsen, you are experts in your field and I'm honored you permitted me to include your work in my book and even made suggestions on the final copy. To all the people who read the book and wrote early testimonials, I appreciate your time, effort, and honest opinions.

This book could not have been possible without the last two years of support from Jenn T. Grace and her team at Publish Your Purpose. Jenn, you are generous, gifted, and a powerhouse. Many thanks to my developmental editor Blue DuLac, who helped shape the book and supported me with her graphic design talents as well. Thanks to Nancy Graham-Tillman, my copy editor who patiently guided me toward the final version of this book. To Chris Agnos, my project manager, thanks for walking me through all the steps to make this book a reality. And a special thanks to Brandi Lai and my classmates Diane, Midge, Julina, and Erin in the PYP writing course, who gave me my very first feedback as I began writing the book. Thanks to the whole PYP writing community who continue to share their experiences in every stage of their publishing journey. I'm honored to join you. To anyone else involved in the success of bringing my book to print, such as proofreaders and typesetters, thank you! It takes a village and PYP provided it.

I couldn't be the person and coach I am today without the following training:

Coaches Training Institute for my foundational coach training; Center for Right Relationships for Organization and Relationship Systems training; David Emerald and Donna Zajonc, founders of the Center for The Empowerment Dynamic*; Millie Grenough, author and founder of *Oasis in the Overwhelm;* and Margaret Greenburg and Senia Maymin, authors of *Profit from the Positive.* Shirzad Chamine's Positive Intelligence program came into my life when the world was shut down in 2020. I was lucky enough to study with a pod of wonderful coaches; Ele, Tanice, Sharon, and Dave, and continued the discussion with Shivani, Lori, Naomi, and Renata.

I must acknowledge the International Coaching Federation, and specifically the Connecticut Chapter, where I was able to grow both personally and professionally. I found a home that served me in many ways, including ongoing training and nurturing my leadership role. I thank each and every member of the board I was honored to serve with over the years, including current and past presidents Judy Garfinkel, Margaret Ruff, Lori Candela, Stephanie Tishler, Dina Markind, Jean Stetz-Puchalski, Steve Porcaro, Sheila Wall, Karin Whitley, Alex Keleman, Carol Shear, and Kathie Nitz. Dina, you're a kindred spirit with the same core values and passion for coaching. Your friendship and continued partnership are invaluable.

I'd like to thank the clients I've had the honor and pleasure to work with, several of whom have given me permission to share parts of their journey on these pages. There is a saying in the coaching world that the universe brings us clients to teach us lessons. I've had overwhelmed clients when I was overwhelmed, relationship clients when I needed to improve my own communication skills, and business clients when I was growing my business. Their wins mirrored my wins, their growth mirrored my growth.

Acknowledgments

I want to acknowledge the many authors who came before me, challenging me to look at the world through a new lens and teaching me to challenge my status quo. Each time I learned something new, I felt like I had a new tool to make my life easier and to share with my clients. There are too many books to list them all, but *The Power of TED**, by David Emerald, challenged me to be a Creator, not a Victim. Thanks to Byron Katie, whose book *Loving What Is,* taught me to question, and not believe my every thought, and thanks to John Gottman, PhD, whose *Seven Principals for Making Marriage Work* gave me relationship tools for all situations. Other authors who influenced my work include Donna Zajonc, Stephen Covey, Rick Hanson, James Clear, Angela Duckworth, Shirzad Chamine, Millie Grenough, Margaret Greenburg, Senia Maymin, Ranye Kaye, Gretchen Rubin, Susan Pierce Thompson, my sister Katherine Dering, and my dear friends Martha Rhodes, and Tanya Detrik. Thank you all.

Finally, I'd like to thank others who have personally supported me on this journey for the last two years. Specifically, to my puzzle group friends, Lorraine, Carol, Juli, Dorothy, Viki, and Amber, we stayed connected through the whole pandemic and continue to puzzle and chat almost weekly. I thank you for the enriching ways you put POP into my life!

DEDICATION

To my children, grandchildren, and husband Steve, I love you more than I can say. You are my guiding light.

To all those who ever feel doubtful, overwhelmed, or stuck, know that your Best Self is inside, ready to be your compass. May your moments of doubt be brief, your moments of clarity, confidence, and decisiveness be plentiful, and may you live your Best Life with joy and ease.

> *Life is a journey, not a destination.*
> —Ralph Waldo Emerson

TABLE OF CONTENTS

Dear Reader xxiii

Part One: It Takes a Shift. 2

Chapter 1: Before and After. 4
    My Before and After. 6
    Plot Your Course 12
    Focus on What You Can Control 14

Chapter 2: Shift from Doubtful to Decisive. 18
    It Takes Many Shifts 19
    Address Challenges 26
    The Road Less Traveled. 29

Chapter 3: Lean into Change. 34
    Commitment, Decisiveness, and Confidence 37

Part Two: Understand Yourself. 48

Chapter 4: Nature, Nurture, and Mindfulness 52
    Nature. 53
    Nurture. 58
    Mindfulness 70
    Forging Paths and Blazing Trails 70
    Acceptance, Compromise, and Adaptation. 75

Chapter 5: Thoughts 78
    Limiting Beliefs 82
    Dial Up, Dial Down. 88
    Fear. 90

    Thoughts. Feelings. Actions. Results. 94
    Noticing Your Mindset. 101

Chapter 6: Inner Self. 106
    Explore Your Inner Parts 107
    A Comparison of Parts Work 112
    Procrastination 121
    Flow. 123

Chapter 7: Our Inner Cast of Characters 130
    Introducing My Cast 135
    Positive Inner Parts 137

Chapter 8: Priorities, Outcomes, and Goals 142
    Priorities. 143
    Outcomes and Goals 147
    Outcome Statements. 148
    Strategies to Accelerate Your Goals 156

Part Three: Take Eight Steps. 168

Step 1: Awareness 172

Step 2: Acceptance. 180

Step 3: Mindset. 186
    Ways to Select an Empowered Mindset 193

Step 4: Assessing 200
    Brainstorming Tools 203

Step 5: Planning. 214

Step 6: Action 226
    Action Steps 227

Step 7: Completion 242
    The Exhilaration of Completion! 247

Step 8: Reflection. 252
    Celebration, Evaluation, and Next Steps 253

    Personal Growth................................ 256
    Lessons Learned............................... 258
    Post-Project Reflections 261

Conclusion... 269

Glossary... 273

References.. 281

About the Author.................................. 287

List of Exercises

Exercise 1: Five Years from Now.................. xxx
Exercise 2: Your Before and After 11
Exercise 3: Write Your Outcome Statement.......... 16
Exercise 4: Focus on What You Want 20
Exercise 5: Make Emotional Shifts 21
Exercise 6: Be Proactive........................... 25
Exercise 7: Overcome Obstacles 27
Exercise 8: Doubtful to Decisive 32
Exercise 9: Commit 41
Exercise 10: Explore Your Confidence 44
Exercise 11: Lean In............................... 45
Exercise 12: Who Have You Always Been?........... 56
Exercise 13: Identify Your Achilles Heels............ 59
Exercise 14: Explore Your Beliefs 64
Exercise 15: Consider Your Values 66
Exercise 16: Recognize Your Habits 69
Exercise 17: Practice Mindfulness 77
Exercise 18: Identify Your Limiting Beliefs 86
Exercise 19: Dial Up, Dial Down 89
Exercise 20: Face Your Fears 93
Exercise 21: Build Your RAFT 98
Exercise 22: Create Your Finest and Best List 101
Exercise 23: Reach Your Inner Parts............... 110
Exercise 24: Recognize Your Saboteurs 120

Exercise 25: Identify Your Parts 127
Exercise 26: Outsmart Your Hindering Parts 134
Exercise 27: Characterize Your Parts 137
Exercise 28: Clear the Path to Your Best Self. 139
Exercise 29: Set Priorities 146
Exercise 30: Write Your Outcome Statement and Goals. . 151
Exercise 31: Explore Your Emotional Goals 152
Exercise 32: Identify Your Goal Patterns 155
Exercise 33: Ease In 160
Exercise 34: Embrace the Person You're Becoming . . . 162
Exercise 35: Maintain Your Goals 166
Exercise 36: Raise Your Awareness 177
Exercise 37: Practice Acceptance (with Reframes). . . . 184
Exercise 38: Set a Decisive Mindset 199
Exercise 39: Assess. 211
Exercise 40: Prepare Your Yes/No List 219
Exercise 41: Pump the Gas or Push the Brakes 223
Exercise 42: Plan 224
Exercise 43: Enjoy the Journey 234
Exercise 44: Become Aware of Your Actions. 239
Exercise 45: Prioritize 247
Exercise 46: Write Your Completion Story 251
Exercise 47: Reflect on Your Personal Growth 257
Exercise 48: Reflect on the Process. 266

> *Go confidently in the direction of your dreams.*
> *Live the life you have imagined.*
>
> —Henry David Thoreau

DEAR READER

Today I want you to think of the compass rose as a symbol for your transformation journey. Each time you see this symbol stop and take three slow, deep breaths. Remember the outcomes you are working toward. Breathe in curiosity and a desire to discover, learn, and grow. As you exhale, release confusion, frustration, and anxiety. Any time you begin to feel stuck or overwhelmed, remember to breathe!

I've written this book for people like me (my younger self, my current self, and every age in between) who have too much doubt in their thoughts and not enough clarity, confidence, and decisiveness to take action. I am the evolving version of you, my ideal reader. For the last fifteen years, I've become more aware of what keeps me stuck and have been creating new ways to be more mindful and intentional about the choices I make. I've taken classes, read books, and tested new ideas and techniques while teaching webinars and coaching clients. It's easier for me to help others see their vulnerabilities and blind spots than to see my own.

This book is something I wish I had twenty years ago when I was driving in circles and repeating the same mistakes, not knowing how to make progress.

I've chosen to live a very flexible life as a home-based professional and hands-on mother and grandmother rather than have a nine-to-five job with predictability and a boss. With all that freedom comes a constant stream of decisions to make and obstacles to overcome—obstacles that are both internal (from me) and external (from the world). My thoughts give me a barrage of "things I must do" and "things I must avoid." My life's circumstances pose the potential for steady interruptions, enticing me to ignore my daily plan in favor of setting other priorities. Family and friends are a constant tug at my heart because connecting with them is my top priority, which puts my business goals and passions far too often at a distant second.

When our values and goals are at odds, we can feel as if we're stuck in the mud, unable to get free and move forward. A racing mind is like a spinning wheel that cannot gain traction. It takes a clear mind to set your course and move forward with focus and direction. How do you get there? I hope this book will be your answer. I'm challenging you to be a detective in your own life—to investigate the way your mind works for you and against you. Look for the patterns when you're at your best and when you struggle the most. Using that insight along with the new tools, concepts, and strategies from this book, you'll be able to shift the way you think, the way you feel, and the action you take.

Before I get into all the tools and strategies, though, I want to share with you a handful of key concepts. I'll be using a few terms with some frequency, so I'd like to define them upfront so that you have a faster uptake of the concepts I'm sharing.

First and foremost is **mindfulness**. I believe that we all have a natural tendency to speed through our day on autopilot. Becoming a mindful driver of our own lives allows us to live with our eyes wide open and our minds ready to move forward. According to Mindful.org (n.d.), "Mindfulness is the basic human ability to be fully present, aware of where we are and what we're doing, and not overly reactive or overwhelmed by what's going on around us." This is one of the keys to success in today's world.

Having a practice of mindfulness is a key step toward being our **Best Self** (the clear-minded version of ourselves) and living our **Best Life** (living what we truly want for all aspects of our life). Like many of you, I've always wanted to be my Best Self, but I didn't know who that was. I just knew it wasn't the **Current Me**. Now I think I know. My Best Self isn't a "someone"; it's an essence that always existed inside of me but was clouded by a stream of sabotaging, doubtful, and confusing thoughts. Confidence isn't enough to help us be our Best Self. We need clarity and direction, and we need to take time to explore the outpouring of thoughts that come from our **inner parts**, the unique subpersonalities of our minds such as our **Avoider, Controller**, or **Indulger**, that are trying to bring our attention to something. Rather than trying to ignore them, we should seek to understand these parts. They'll eventually lose their urgency and become an accepted part of us.

We all have many inner parts—aspects of ourselves that each have their own goals, intentions, and thoughts. For instance, the Worrier tries to keep us safe, the Avoider stays away from anything difficult or uncomfortable, and the Indulger tries to make us happy when we've had a rough day. Surely, a part of you picked up this book because it felt hopeful while another part of you felt hopeless. There are as many parts to us as there are emotions, and each part evolves from the time we're children to the time we go through something traumatic, scary, or new.

These parts of us can be helpful, but they can also distract or derail us from our intentions. Their ever-present thoughts need to be filtered out to find what's true and what's a story our psyches are making up. Parts live in the same region of our brain as our memories. They can show up like clockwork every time we think we have a great idea or want to pursue something new: *Oh, no you don't! You're going to fail just like the last time you tried something like that.* I'll bet you've heard a recent message from an inner part trying to convince you that there's no point in trying to learn and grow: *You are who you are, and you might as well get used to it!* Perhaps the Champion part is trying to convince you to try: *You can do it. There is hope that you can get unstuck, and this time will be different.* I hope you'll listen to that Champion voice. There's much more in this book to guide you in that direction. There is hope!

The more you can live as your Best Self, the sooner you can live your Best Life. This year's idealized version of your Best Life might be the reality of your life five years from now. To step into your new future, the one you envision for yourself, you need to shift your old way of thinking and being. It's up to you to get curious, explore, and make conscious changes to get new results.

The Action Cycle

I want to give you a sneak preview of the **Action Cycle**. It's a tool I created over ten years ago with a coaching friend of mine, Anna Cole. The tool, like me and my coaching, has evolved over the years. At its core, the Action Cycle is a step-by-step process to help you overcome obstacles and guide you toward taking purposeful and intentional action. The eight steps are Awareness, Acceptance, Mindset, Assessing, Planning, Action, Completion, and Reflection.

Once you identify a specific challenge, you're ready to use the Action Cycle. I go more deeply into each of the steps in "Take Eight Steps," the third section of this book, and I've provided a brief description of them below. The Awareness step is the key to exploring your issue, recognizing the reality of your circumstances, defining the outcome you want, and identifying the obstacles that are standing in your way. Most of this book is designed to raise your Awareness. The rest of the steps will help you get into the right **Mindset** to set intentions and take Action. Each of the eight steps builds on the previous one and sets you up to achieve your desired results.

1. **Awareness**: Something isn't quite right, and you'd like to seek change. Use this step to explore what's going on, both the obvious and the not-so-obvious.
2. **Acceptance**: You know that to see change, you have to let go of what isn't working. You can't control everything, but you can control the choices you make and accept responsibility for your own actions.
3. **Mindset**: Your Mindset is your perspective or frame of mind about your issue, problem, or circumstance. By focusing on the goals you want to achieve with an open mind instead of using problem-centered thinking, you can find motivation for and commitment to making changes.
4. **Assessing**: Weigh the options available to resolve your challenge, explore the possibilities without hesitation, and recruit support if needed.
5. **Planning**: Accelerate your execution by creating a plan with the best options available for you to gain clarity, focus, and direction.

6. **Action**: Choose Action over distraction to keep moving forward. Realize the compounding effect of every tiny step along the way.
7. **Completion**: Keep committing yourself to your goal each day to reach your destination.
8. **Reflection**: Take time to notice where you've come from and where you ended up. Don't forget to celebrate your growth. You can choose to maintain this goal or select another challenge to overcome by going back to Awareness to start a new cycle.

The Action Cycle is just that—a cyclical process that brings you from the Awareness that you have an idea or issue to deal with, all the way to the Completion or resolution of your issue and Reflection of the process. Awareness and Reflection happen throughout the cycle—they're both about knowing, learning, and noticing. Whenever you learn something new or your status changes, you may have to adjust your plan and start Assessing all over again. That's okay. At least that way you understand where you are in the cycle and can get right back in the game.

Using the Action Cycle

If you don't want to stay stuck with the same old **habits** giving you the same old results, you can use the Action Cycle to gain insight, address issues in new ways, create new strategies, and develop new habits. Start with smaller challenges that may allow you to breeze through the steps in a few minutes. Work your way up to more complicated and/or emotion-charged challenges that may take more time and effort.

My goal for you is that reading this book and doing the associated "work" will allow you to create a firm foundation.

From there you can achieve your Best Self and your Best Life, based on what you really want. Take the time to paint your before and after pictures. Learn about the shifts required to make lifelong changes. Get to know yourself better, including your inner parts, and learn strategies and tools to set priorities and achieve goals. When you reach the Action Cycle, you'll be ready to jump right in and transform your life, one issue and one goal at a time. You'll no longer feel doubtful or stuck, at least not for any length of time. You'll have the tools and insights to stop doubt in its tracks and choose a mindful solution with intention and confidence.

A few tips as you read the book:

❖ I've bolded important words and phrases the first time I use them, and you can find a definition for each of them in the glossary at the back of the book.

❖ I've used italics when giving an example of an inner thought or Mindset and have capitalized the words representing each of the eight steps of the Action Cycle any time they're mentioned.

❖ Throughout the book, I've included many exercises for journaling (you can find a summary of these on my website as well). I encourage you to use a journal or notebook to record your thoughts and work through exercises as you read the book. The community at MonicaLeggett.com can offer support along the way and provide additional worksheets.

Exercise 1: Five Years from Now...

Imagine it's five years from now and you've been on a "personal development" journey, using the Action Cycle and all the associated strategies. You've been paying attention to your thoughts and using them to make choices, take Action, and get the results you want. You're living a life of balance and joy, which includes meaningful work and time for play. You know what you like, you follow your heart, and you've achieved a much better level of self-care with healthy goals and boundaries. You're at relative ease when you're called to address personal decisions, external issues, or family drama.

Here are a few questions to ponder as you consider that state while reading this book:

1. What do you want?
2. What issue(s) do you want to work through to make that happen?
3. What will you stop doing, start doing, or let go of to accelerate your goals?
4. What is the biggest shift you need to make to improve your life?

It's time to make things happen!

Monica

PART ONE
It Takes a Shift

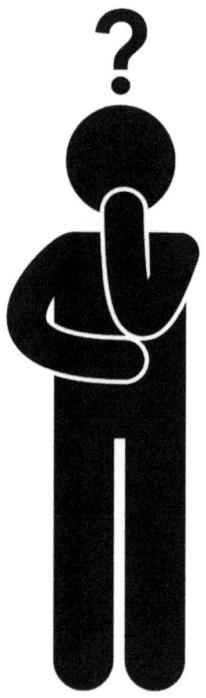

> *To exist is to change, to change is to mature, to mature is to go on creating oneself endlessly.*
>
> —Henri-Louis Bergson, *Creative Evolution*

Part 1: It Takes a Shift

Chapter 1: Before and After
Chapter 2: Shift from Doubtful to Decisive
Chapter 3: Lean into Change

We can embrace many shifts on the way to a more empowered, successful, and happy life. Just knowing that we're making a shift is a good start. We're leaving the beaten path behind and steering in a new direction. Once we do that, the opportunities are endless. Our focus will change, our emotions will lift, and our results will be dramatic. Each change we embrace takes time and effort and requires a shift of expectation that this isn't a quick fix but a lifelong journey.

Patterns before the Shift	**New experiences after the Shift**
Doubtful, ineffective, stressed	Decisive, effective, at ease
Problem-focused	Desired outcome-focused
Do it alone	Invite outside support
Avoid and dread challenges	Identify and deal with challenges
Be reactive, automatic	Be proactive, mindful
Same behavior, same results	Intentional behavior, new results
Resisting change	Accepting and owning change

CHAPTER 1
BEFORE AND AFTER

> *You have sole custody of your life.*
> *Who you are today is not who you have to be tomorrow.*
> *Embrace the possibility of transformation.*
>
> —Leeza Gibbons

- ➢ My Before and After
- ➢ Plot Your Course
- ➢ Focus on What You Can Control

Think about your life. Do you struggle to make decisions or overcome challenges as you go about your life? What if things could be different?

Imagine being faced with a challenge to overcome and instead of procrastinating and being held back by feelings of indecisiveness, confusion, and self-doubt, you feel confident. You have a process to face challenges head-on with clarity and to take decisive Action. You feel motivated to complete tasks and projects and find ease and **flow** in your existence. Your life is free from hesitation and full of purpose and balance—you have found your Best Life.

I propose that this life is possible. Think of it as your future life, your destination.

- ❖ You prioritize, address, delegate, or dismiss tasks one at a time.
- ❖ You put on your calm mediator hat to resolve conflicts.
- ❖ You find a way to bring your big ideas to life.
- ❖ You gather the facts, check in with your gut, reach out to your favorite supporters, and feel good about your decisions.

Stephen Covey, author of *7 Habits of Highly Effective People* might describe this visualization as "begin[ning] with the end in mind" (1989, 95–144). In our mind's eye, we create an image of the person we want to become or the outcome we want to achieve, a person living by the values that we deem most important. Then we step outside of our minds to begin our journey. However, visualization isn't enough. The bigger the change you want to make, the more a shift in your way of thinking, being, and doing is required. This takes time, practice, and a long-term commitment.

> **It takes a million little steps to see big changes.**

Only you can define your Best Self and your Best Life. There's no shortcut, no magic wand, no futuristic portal to take you there. You know better than anyone what challenges you face and goals you want to achieve. By reading this book, you're taking the first step of your journey. Figure out what you want and take one mindful Action at a time to get you there. Take, for example, my own before-and-after journey.

My Before and After

My husband, Steve, wanted to move in 2006, but I was on the fence. We had been in our home for over thirteen years and had done many projects that transformed the house. We opened walls, did a kitchen and bathroom makeover that belonged in a magazine, and put on a new roof and siding. Steve created beautiful landscaping with gardens, retaining walls, a gazebo, a deck, and a stone patio. Stone carvings became a water feature, and rock walls became an obstacle course for the local chipmunks to scamper through. It sounds idyllic, but the problem was that it was never our "dream home." There were many limitations, including a small lot without privacy. Unfortunately, none of our renovations could change that.

That summer, I had an opportunity to go to a three-day training class with my older sister, Grace. It was the perfect opportunity to spend some time together since we lived on opposite ends of the country. Little did I know that my time there would change the trajectory of my life. She was the co-instructor, and I was curious about her profession of **coaching**. During the training, I had the opportunity to be coached by a classmate. The topic I chose was my possible move. It weighed on me that my husband wasn't happy where we lived. Plus, I wanted some clarity and a resolution to get off the fence and take Action to find peace.

Three Versions of the Story

1. **Reality:** Steve and I have three adult children and a beautiful two-story cape house that, although previously stuck in the fifties, we had transformed into a showstopper. We've been happy raising our children here, but it isn't perfect. After all the updates I'm satisfied, but Steve is still looking for his dream home.
2. **Steve's Story:** "The problem is that the yard is very small, and we have no privacy. I work very long days commuting into New York City, and I'm surrounded by swing sets and young kids, making it difficult to enjoy my yard on the weekends. I've been going to open houses for years, and sometimes Monica comes with me. I truly believe our 'dream home' is out there."

3. **My Story:** "I don't want to leave this house! After all that work to turn our house into a beautiful home, how could we leave? Besides, I'll have to purge, pack, make arrangements for the dog every time we show the house, and work my part-time job while my husband will be gone fourteen hours a day. I'll have to leave my neighbors, and I love my house—it's beautifully updated, and the yard is magical! This is stressing me out!"

The Coaching Process

My novice coach asked me a series of questions and then helped me explore the issue. In that twenty-minute session, I realized that if I wanted to move or stay, I needed to gather some concrete information. What is our house worth? What could we buy that would be better? How would the financial changes impact our budget? Before I could make a decision, I had to know the facts and imagine what was possible beyond the selling process. Instead of focusing on what we could gain, I was focusing on what I believed would be the painful process of selling our home.

However, as I thought more about it, I realized that I had seen homes that offered more than our current one. Keeping that in mind, I allowed my Adventurer to begin to emerge as I developed a plan with my coach.

❖ Phase 1: Create a list of questions to ask the professionals. If I felt comfortable with the answers, I could confidently agree to put the house on the market.

❖ Phase 2: Work with Steve to purge, pack, and move any excess items into storage. That way we'd have a less cluttered space, which shows better to potential buyers. As we get ready to sell, we can interview three realtors and pick our favorite to list our home.
❖ Phase 3: Embrace finding our dream home!

Using the support of coaching to figure out what I wanted to do allowed me to create a plan to present to Steve. All I had to do was ask, and I'd have a good partner to help me through the process. I didn't have to bear the full weight of the move on my own. I realized that I was willing to move if the opportunity presented itself.

My Mindset used to be:

This is too hard.

After coaching, it shifted to:

I have clarity and a plan! I'm ready to explore what is possible instead of focusing on my challenges. I'm ready to let go of all the wrong reasons to stay, and I'm ready to explore our options. My home could use a little purging and organization so, whether we move or not, it will be worth the effort.

Did you hear the shift in my thoughts? That **reframe**—a shift from a problem-focused Mindset to a desired outcome-focused Mindset—was so important for me. Instead of getting stuck, I found a new perspective on solving challenges. This allowed me to get excited rather than feel like a victim. I was no longer caught in a plot to unravel my happiness, casting my husband as the persecutor for suggesting we move.

What I got from that coaching session was rather miraculous for me, but not abnormal for coaching and consistent with the coaching process. My decisive Mindset came from the clarity I had gained, and that came from Acceptance, belief, and commitment—the Acceptance to address the issue rather than ignore it, the belief that we would either find something better or stay where we were, and the commitment to follow the plan.

The house went on the market in July, a month after my coaching class. It was sold in August, and we moved into our dream home in September. The first moment we saw the house it took our breath away. We couldn't believe we could own such a beautiful property. It had over one and a half acres with mature gardens and trees, a three-car garage (ideal for Steve's woodshop), and plenty of privacy from the neighbors. We still live in our dream home over seventeen years later.

Initially, I was thankful to have found a new approach to solving challenging issues. On a much deeper level, I learned about my thought process and the old habits that no longer served me. I had been avoiding, procrastinating, and deferring to the future, which resulted in making the present a painful place to exist. Now, I've learned to work through my discomfort, by myself or with a supporter, in so many areas of my life. By releasing the old me and continuing to embrace the ever-evolving me—someone who focuses on what she wants and quiets the voice of the problem-focused naysayer—I've moved closer to my Best Self.

It has taken more than just this one event to find out who I really am, and my journey didn't end there. The old me still lingers and is most prevalent when life is chaotic or when dealing with obstacles. It still takes effort to stay mindful of all the old habits and choose a different path. Yet now when I face an issue or ponder a new goal, I rarely sit in doubt and avoidance for very long. By asking myself some key questions, I can push past the old default responses that don't get me where I want to go, and I can reframe my thoughts. When I stop protecting the status quo, I find myself becoming more decisive and taking more Action toward goals that are meaningful to me.

Exercise 2: Your Before and After

Now it's your turn. Be bold. Paint a picture of your own before and after. Take a piece of paper and draw a line down the center from top to bottom. Label the left half "Before" and the right half "After." Fill in each side using these prompts and questions to guide you:

1. Describe your current life (your before picture).
   - → What's here now that works for you, and what's here that doesn't?
   - → What feels incomplete or in need of attention?
   - → What are you doing now that you'd like to do more of? Less of?
2. Describe what your life will be like in six months or five years (your after picture).
   - → What do you want?
   - → What is possible if you focus on what's important to you?

→ What is your reality? Make statements in the present tense, such as in the examples below.
  ❖ I exercise five times a week, including walks with friends and at least once a week with weights.
  ❖ I have a thriving business with _____ steady clients, _____ income, and a virtual assistant to support all my marketing and billing.
→ What aspects of your life are most important to you? Describe them all in detail (e.g., health, home, family, relationships, finances, career).

3. Write statements that describe who you've become.
   → What are the new qualities of your life?
   → What are your new character traits?
     ❖ I am the person who _____.

Fill in the blank over and over again using different traits.

Plot Your Course

To plot any journey on a map, we must first identify where we are (Point A) and where we want to go (Point B). It's the same with setting intentions and achieving goals. We need to set aside time for Reflection and gain a deep Awareness of our current situations, our priorities, and our desired outcomes. We then need to assess ways to achieve our goals as well as prepare for any challenges that might stand in our way. We can use the Action Cycle to overcome them. Deciding what we want defines our destination.

Not everyone has a big gap between Point A and Point B; they may be closer than you think. Perhaps you feel calm, happy, and proud of yourself most of the time and are looking to make one little shift. That tiny shift might be what changes your entire life. You don't need to move mountains; you only need to move in the direction that gets you closer to what you want.

When taking this journey, identify and focus on your destination. Be present, and try not to judge the difficulty of your journey before you've even started or you may never get out of neutral. While you may experience many forks and detours along the way, the road could also be relatively straight and have only minor speed bumps. You can't know until you begin. Keep reminding yourself of the reason for the journey, and return to the Action Cycle whenever you need support. Be sure to celebrate your accomplishments, no matter how big or small. Every little step keeps your engine running. You'll never find your Best Life if you stall out before you get there.

Problems and challenges show up in all areas of our lives. Jessica and her boyfriend, for example, have worked and lived together for several years. Their desired outcome was to solve a relationship dilemma. Aware that they never had time off to enjoy their life together, one would burn out, force themselves to take a few days off, and then feel guilty sitting in the garden while the other worked. After Assessing their options, they finally decided to block out four days a month when neither would work. It has changed their lives in so many ways. They set an intentional boundary to protect their time off and have been able to keep it going for almost a year. Their only regret is that they didn't make this shift sooner.

FOCUS ON WHAT YOU CAN CONTROL

As you experience life's journey, let go of the illusion of control, and allow things to come and go. There will always be unexpected obstacles and setbacks, so stop fretting over their potential existence. There will also be wins when you move forward after a bump. Appreciate both, learn what you can, and take that knowledge on your journey.

Keep moving forward. With each revolution of the Action Cycle starting at a new level of Awareness and ending with the next level of Action, the journey may feel a little cyclical. Reflection brings you back to new Awareness, bringing you higher and higher toward your Best Self and your Best Life. Just remember to be patient. Rushing may pile on so many obstacles at once that you might become overwhelmed. Take one step at a time. Allow yourself the time to go from Point A to Point B, and collect lessons along the way to smooth your future journeys. With patience, practice, and commitment to your journey, you will be able to:

- ❖ release old habits and limiting beliefs,
- ❖ rewrite the stories you tell yourself,
- ❖ recognize and accept all parts of yourself, and
- ❖ resolve to intentionally pursue what you want.

These changes will shift your daily actions and bring you new results. In the end, you'll have the potential to be a new version of yourself, with new habits, systems, and self-care with more ease and flow in your life. You'll feel pride in the decisive choices you make and celebrate when you overcome challenges and complete goals. With practice, you'll change your wiring and more often experience life as your Best Self.

To realize this shift, you need to start with foundational skills, which I hope this book will provide you. As you continue to practice, your identity will change. You'll add habits that support you in becoming the best version of yourself. You'll become what you want to be and achieve the goals you desire. Perhaps you'll become more organized, decisive, or accepting of others. Maybe you'll confidently assume new roles as a thought leader or excel in your business. By bringing together all the things you want, you converge them into your new way of being. At first it may seem like hard work, but eventually you'll find that it's just who you are and how you exist.

The typical self-help book, workshop, and advice column tries to teach you one thing: how to fix a specific issue, hone a particular skill, or see a new perspective. One problem with this approach is that it's too easy to slip back into our old ways of being. We've adjusted only one puzzle piece, and the others want to find equilibrium by going back to their old states. The best way to find balance and keep up with the new instead of falling back on the old is by using a **holistic approach**. This approach encompasses all our parts—the things we're best at as well as the things we find challenging. A holistic approach uses all parts of the Action Cycle, too, including the Awareness to notice the need for a change, the Mindset to help us get there, the Action to make even small changes in our lives, and the Reflection that helps us assimilate what we've learned and guides our next steps.

When we do the work to understand ourselves and each other, we gain insight that lasts a lifetime. This allows our Best Self to take Action without hesitation, commit through to Completion, and take the time for Reflection on the process. It helps us see what to celebrate, maintain, and build upon.

There will always be setbacks that knock us down for a little while. Yet, with every challenge we overcome and every problem we solve, we have the opportunity to get back up with a new skill, strategy, or insight added to our identity. We

become more focused, persistent, and resilient. As a result, we may joyfully find ourselves making statements like these:
I am the person who ...

- ❖ overcame a challenge.
- ❖ failed and then tried again.
- ❖ set up a new routine, developed a new habit, and then kept it going!

Exercise 3: Write Your Outcome Statement

Think about what you desire and who you desire to be. What are the outcomes you want? Paint your "after" picture by writing at least one outcome statement as if it has already happened, following this format: *I am the person who ...*
Here are some examples:

- ❖ *I am the person who* found the job I've always wanted.
- ❖ *I am the person who* hosted a family gathering without any drama.
- ❖ *I am the person who* published a book and sold 10,000 copies in the first year!

Add plenty of details to your statement and let your mind dream.

CHAPTER 2
SHIFT FROM DOUBTFUL TO DECISIVE

> *You should never view your challenges as a disadvantage. Instead, it's important for you to understand that your experience facing and overcoming adversity is actually one of your biggest advantages.*
>
> —Michelle Obama

- ➤ It Takes Many Shifts
- ➤ Address Challenges
- ➤ The Road Less Traveled

Before you begin any project, you may already be experiencing doubtful thoughts about the challenges you're facing. Thoughts like these will cloud your decision-making process in addition to preventing you from looking for solutions and taking Action:

- ❖ *What if I can't figure this out? Should I even bother?*
- ❖ *I don't know how I'm going to get all this done. Where do I start?*
- ❖ *What is the next career step—do I explore that risky opportunity?*
- ❖ *I don't think this is the right time to have that difficult conversation.*
- ❖ *Why would it work this time? It hasn't before.*

Small shifts in the way you think, prioritize your time, and approach life will move you away from doubt and toward a decisive life. Making one small shift at a time can take you to a new destination. No matter how small the shift, it will keep you moving forward.

It Takes Many Shifts

The first and most significant shift may seem obvious: **shift from focusing on the problem to focusing on the outcome you want.** Yet we often struggle to make that shift. As you saw in my before and after story, having a problem-focused Mindset leads to doubts and feeling stuck. It puts your mind on a downward spiral that sees no possibilities and creates stories about all the negative potential outcomes. An outcome focus, on the other hand, lets your mind fill in the hopeful blanks, helping you feel motivated to take even the smallest steps.

Exercise 4: Focus on What You Want

This is an exercise to dissuade doubt from taking up residence in your mind. Being mindful can help keep you focused on where you're going instead of on how things could go wrong along the way. When you ask yourself what you want or need to live your Best Life, follow these steps:

- Lift your chin high, and open up your posture.
- Take a few slow, deep breaths.
- Remember that you want something and that you can do something about it.
- Ask the Doubtful part of you to step aside for a little while.
- Allow the confident and curious parts of you to explore what you want and what it could look like for you in the future.
- Focus on your curiosity. Ask yourself, *What is possible?*
- Explore your options from a confident Mindset.

I'm going to explain more about Mindsets in a later chapter, but for now, take a look at these examples of thoughts that support goals:

- *This is the time to set change in motion.*

- ❖ *Progress, not perfection.*
- ❖ *I'm worth it.*

The second shift is to **think about why you want something**. There's a good reason your mind wants some resolution or change—perhaps a value that you want to align with. Spend a little time thinking about what life would be like if you pursued this change rather than staying put. No one wants to feel regret over unchosen paths and missed opportunities.

The third shift is to **stay in the present with an open mind**. Worrying about past or future struggles causes you to feel stuck and prevents you from taking steps toward your desired outcomes. *Why bother? I've tried it before, and it didn't work* becomes *I'll try something a little different this time.* This is an example of reframing, or looking at the same situation in a new way. Be present in the here and now, with a fresh perspective, and explore the possibilities that lie ahead of you. Notice what energizes you and what drains you, what makes you feel happy, and what is utterly frustrating. Use that information to guide you toward what you want more or less of in the future.

Exercise 5: Make Emotional Shifts

Spend five minutes a day reflecting on the way you feel and then do something about it. If you're feeling great, then do more of whatever you're doing! If not, name your emotion, and see if there's a little shift you can make to change your situation. Be proactive, and you'll see a shift in your mood.

1. Do you feel stressed? What is one thing you can do to take care of yourself?

2. Do you feel unworthy? Focus on something you're proud of—no matter how small.
3. Do you feel overwhelmed? Break down your tasks into smaller chunks and start with one step.

It takes a shift in your thinking to see a shift in your results.

Act Intentionally

Society expects us to do so much, day in and day out. While busy, you may not be as content as you hope. Are the things you spend time on adding to your life and feeding your soul? Do you feel energized or drained? **Becoming intentional and proactive rather than reactive** is the fourth shift that can help shape your Best Life.

Being intentionally active means evaluating how you're using your time while making intentional, mindful choices. You're present to your circumstances, you choose to address nagging problems rather than skip over issues that may need your attention, and you plan out your approach rather than making reactive choices based on default habits, avoidance, or pleasing others. That approach may make you feel stuck, like a car spinning its tires in the mud, or overwhelmed and unsatisfied by your results.

- → Do you ever regret your actions or inactions?
- → Could you be happier by resolving glaring issues you've ignored?
- → Do you avoid or downplay your priorities?

I'm asking you to break through the automatic cycle of thinking and acting that leads you down the same old path. Stop to get centered and reflect on your current reality. Use the opportunity to make small changes that make a big difference. Focus your attention on important personal and professional goals. Then take planned Action to achieve those goals so you can get to Completion and Reflection.

Pay attention and be intentional.

I'm the first person to admit I sometimes get stuck. Most recently, I got stuck while writing this book and selecting the title. How ironic! Still, even with doubts, I persisted by taking proactive, decisive Action and committing myself to my goal every day. I organized my thoughts, set aside time to write, and worked with experts to finish my book. However, it took more than those daily commitments to accomplish my goal. I had a few other key strategies in my pocket:

- ❖ **Support and Training**: I enrolled in a six-month writing program for nonfiction writers under the guidance of Jenn T. Grace, a professional editor and publisher. One of the added benefits was finding my writing buddy, Midge.

- ❖ **Structure**: I established weekly slots on my calendar devoted to writing and attending meetings that supported my book-writing goal.
- ❖ **Deadlines**: I set deadlines for different steps of the book.
- ❖ **Accountability**: I worked with Midge, coaching colleagues, and my publishing team at Publish Your Purpose to keep me on target.

Support, training, structure, deadlines, and accountability are some of the many things we can have and do to accomplish our goals. What other strategies can you think of that might work for you? The secret to completing a long project is to shift away from doing it on your own and setting unrealistic expectations. Instead, create a plan that includes ways to support your body, mind, and soul until you've crossed the finish line. The more structure and accountability you put in place, the easier your commitment becomes.

Be Proactive

> *Don't sit down and wait for the opportunities to come. Get up and make them.*
>
> —Madam C. J. Walker

According to the *Oxford English Dictionary*, being proactive means "Creating or controlling a situation by taking the initiative and anticipating events or problems, rather than just reacting to them after they have occurred." Being proactive is slightly different from being intentional. Every day, you have the choice to wait for things to happen *to* you or to make them happen *for* you. You can choose to practice gratitude, learn a new skill, or even set boundaries to protect your time and peace of mind. Whenever something isn't contributing to the flow and ease of your Best Life, stop and take notice. Figure out what needs to shift, what is missing, or what you want to let go of. Perhaps one small change will make you feel better. You can also be proactive about letting go of old goals and tasks that no longer support the life you want to lead. Replace them with new, more resonant goals and tasks that support you in living your Best Life.

Exercise 6: Be Proactive

1. What goal would you like to be more proactive about?
2. What would you like to proactively release from your life?
3. How can you increase your intention to make these things happen?

Eliminate Multitasking and Set Boundaries

There are two last shifts I'd like to suggest: **practice a singular focus rather than multitasking**, and **set boundaries with yourself and others so that your priorities remain intact**.

Multitasking helps me get more done is a big myth. You can get many things done in a day, but not if you try to do them all at once. Prioritize your daily or weekly goals and focus on one thing at a time. I also suggest limiting any big projects to one at a time or just a few per quarter. If your mind is trying to work on too many things at once, it becomes a less efficient machine—just like your computer running too many programs at once.

Setting boundaries—what you will allow and what you won't—will free you from all the uncomfortable, wishy-washy arguments you have with yourself. Set clear boundaries, share them with others, and, if you must, design them together with others. Your family and friends can become your biggest allies rather than your constant distractions. This became urgently clear during the pandemic. Many of us were working from home while fighting for quiet spaces and balancing who'd take care of kids' schooling, along with other new roles and responsibilities. I'm sure there were new boundaries introduced to the relationship system or, if there weren't, perhaps you missed an opportunity. Boundaries can feel like stern rules, but in reality they're helpful guidelines that make decision-making easier.

Address Challenges

Each of us will face challenges throughout our lives, but some of us learn to overcome them while others don't. The difference between these two groups of people is that the group that succeeds doesn't ignore or hide from their challenges but looks for ways around or through them, or to learn from them. It doesn't matter whether the challenges are within us, such as our thoughts and worries, or beyond us, such as a demand from our family. Deciding to address challenges already puts the successful group ahead of those who avoid or ignore challenges. Changing the way we deal with them can produce powerful, long-lasting results.

One challenging obstacle we create for ourselves is our problem-focused thoughts, which can leave us feeling stuck and doubtful. We may regret the past, fear the future, and judge the steps we or others have taken. I, too, have slowed my own journey with my doubt, procrastination, and indecisiveness, which has kept me from reaching my full potential. Instead of judging ourselves for being stuck, we need to stop and notice, be honest with ourselves, and ask where mindful Awareness and intentional effort could make our lives shine.

As a life coach for fifteen years and a recovering Procrastinator, I've experienced that getting to understand myself deeply (with all my self-imposed obstacles) has been the key to making lasting change. Don't get stuck in overthinking and focusing on the negative. Instead, reframe your thoughts and learn how to shift as they come and go. If you can point out the challenge, you can be strategic about how to overcome it.

Challenges are inevitable. Accept that and plan for them. When an issue seemingly can't be resolved smoothly, stop and take a good look at why. Most people have a good sense of their biggest struggles, but they may give up before finding a solution. Knowing our obstacles won't eliminate them, but dealing with them can help us get back in control. For example, when you're not doing something, is it because of a lack of time or are you procrastinating or avoiding conflict? Perhaps you don't necessarily lack the time you need but are just hesitating because you aren't sure where to start.

Exercise 7: Overcome Obstacles

Everyone has their own challenges and unique struggles. At the core of each challenge are some obstacles to overcome. You can use this fill-in-the-blank statement to shift toward a solution:

1. [Name your obstacle]. I have [something I want to change], and I want [this instead].

   Examples:
   - ❖ My office is a mess. I have papers everywhere, and I want to be organized instead.

- My team is struggling. They need hand-holding, and I want them to take more initiative.
- My writing has stalled, and I feel stuck. I have five incomplete pieces, and I want to finish them.

2. Part two of this exercise is to brainstorm the reasons why you haven't already resolved the issue. It's an opportunity to shed light on your self-imposed obstacles. As you write down your reasons, ask yourself whether they're actually true or not and out of your control or not.

Using the first of the examples above, your response might look like this:

My office is a mess. I believe that organization is not my strength. Truth be told, I don't take the time to put things away or create a useful system. I rush from task to task and don't prioritize orderliness. I fear that if I put things away, I'll forget about them or forget where they are.

Are your reasons true, or are they simply ways you're throwing up roadblocks to your success? Every goal requires time to make the shifts needed to accomplish it. If it's important enough, you can find the time. Will you?

1. If you could snap your fingers and solve one challenge, what would it be?
2. What roadblock are you putting up that hinders your reaching success?
3. How might you overcome that roadblock?
4. Where in your week can you make time to address this?

THE ROAD LESS TRAVELED

Imagine you're taking a road trip. You know your destination, and you've figured out the best route to get there. Suddenly, after making good progress, a detour takes you off the highway onto a country road you've never traveled before. Within minutes it begins to rain so hard your windshield wipers can't keep up. It becomes difficult to see the road ahead. A deer runs in front of your vehicle, and you barely avoid a collision as you swerve onto the soft shoulder. You bring the car to a stop and begin to lament over all your bad luck. Nothing seems to be going your way.

As you put the car back into drive, you realize that you're now stuck in the mud! Pressing hard on the gas, your wheels spin, but you get no traction. Doing more of the same only digs you deeper into the mud. Putting the car into park, you take a few minutes to breathe and calm yourself. Even with your bad luck, there's a lot to be thankful for; cell service, a working engine, and enough gas in the tank to reach your destination.

Just as you begin contemplating a way to get out of this mess, the rain stops, giving you a new sense of hope. You decide to call your mechanic friend and ask for advice on how to get out of the mud. After following his instructions, you're soon back on solid ground. Checking your smartphone directions, you see that you'll be on the highway again in only a few miles. As you shift into forward gear, you resume your drive, reflecting on what went well and what you learned along the way. You're thankful that you were able to find calm after losing your cool, get help from a friend, and trust your own ability to overcome unexpected obstacles.

Despite everything, this was a win. You learned something about yourself that you can carry forward on your journey: you are resilient! Detours and bad weather will not sour your determination to commit to and achieve your goals.

Let's take a look under the hood to see what each of the elements in this story represents. Your destination represents your desired outcome, or what you want to achieve. The original route you set out with was your plan, or how you were going to reach your goal. The detour, mud, and deer on the road represent the obstacles you experienced as you pursued your goal. Outside of the story, other obstacles could include shortened deadlines, extra costs, or even illness.

Shifting your Mindset is like adjusting a car's transmission. When your mind is jaded, fearful, or muddied by challenging thoughts, you may find yourself stuck in reverse. From there you may choose to stay in park, perhaps finding calm and recharging before you head out again. If your Mindset is positive, curious, open, and focused on the goal that lies ahead, then your car is in drive and you're moving forward.

Which way of thinking might get you closer to your goal: *Step by step I will get there*, or *I will never accomplish my goal*? Remember how important your Mindset is for continuing forward momentum. Your Mindset can be greatly impacted by your mood, just like the weather in our story. Do you have a sunny disposition, or do the smallest obstacles feel like an unexpected downpour? Being mindful of your thoughts and how you interpret challenges can either slow your journey, speed you on your way, or keep you stuck.

Getting out of the mud represents the changes required to free yourself from obstacles. As you peel back the stories and thoughts holding you in place, you'll be able to challenge and replace them with ones that are more aligned with what you want. We all have internal **Saboteurs** such as the Avoider, the Stickler, the Controller, or the Pleaser. Their voices can steal our moving-forward Mindset, muddy our view, and turn our thoughts into a weapon against us. Thankfully, as these naysayers pop up, we can simply allow our wiper blades to scrape them off our windshields, clearing our field of view. Our secret weapon is reframing our thoughts and taking a new approach to solving a problem.

As with any journey, the best way to get to your desired outcome is with a map. In this case, the **MAP** is a combination of your Mindset, the options you're Assessing, and the Planning you do. These are Steps 3, 4, and 5 of the Action Cycle. You determined your best route and are on your way to your destination. Remember, every goal may require a new MAP. Without a clear destination, or by randomly completing goals back and forth throughout the countryside, your car may run out of gas.

In our story, the driver turned to their mechanic friend for advice. While achieving a goal is often possible on your own, turning to supporters sometimes results in more successful outcomes. Who do you turn to? Is it your own wisdom, a mentor, a coach, or a friend? Having a coach-like person in your life who listens and helps you gain clarity is extremely valuable. They don't try to rescue you by telling you what to do. Instead, they act as a sounding board, as well as a brainstorming and accountability partner. They remind you of your commitment to yourself, your values, and your goals. They **model** compassion, courage, confidence, and decisiveness so that you can dial them up within yourself.

When we choose to rely on our wisdom, we have a built-in guide: our Best Self. When you're feeling most challenged, remember to pause (put your car in park), breathe (add some gas to your tank), and trust that your Best Self is there to guide you. Whenever you're stuck, think less about how you arrived in this muddy mess in the first place and more about how you're going to get back on the road to your destination. (You can do a quick Reflection and move on.) Think of how many more miles you can travel when you have enough gas in the car (or charged electric batteries), a good transmission that keeps you moving forward, and a clear vision with no obstacles or bugs on your windshield. Don't try to keep driving when you can't see where you're going.

Exercise 8: Doubtful to Decisive

Now it's your turn to go from doubtful to decisive. Choose one category to focus on first. It could be your health, finances, business/career growth, retirement, family, relationships, free time, fun, stress management, time management, organization of your space, or a different category of your choosing.

1. What area of your life is screaming for attention?
2. Name the specific outcomes you want.
3. What are the challenges you might face that make you feel doubtful?
4. If you were sure it would work out, what steps might you take?
5. Who or what can support you in achieving your goal?
6. What is the most significant shift that would allow you to get your desired outcome?

CHAPTER 3
LEAN INTO CHANGE

> *Change is the law of life.*
> *And those who look only to the past or present are*
> *certain to miss the future.*
>
> —John F. Kennedy

 ➤ Commitment, Decisiveness, and Confidence

Whether we're a student or the founder of a multi-million-dollar company, we all must accept and adapt to change many times over the course of our lives. Change is a necessary aspect of life. We can have change forced upon us, or we can choose to change willingly and with intention. The more mindfully we choose how to change, the more control we have over the shape of our lives and emotions. Resisting change, especially necessary change, can make us feel hopeless, victimized, or out of control. Instead of thinking of change as something to dread, it's helpful to lean in and see what we want to get out of it. Change can be a good thing!

There are many stages to making a change. The **Transtheoretical Model** of behavior change is one of my favorite resources to use when discussing change. It's also known as the **Stages of Change Model** because it recognizes that we go through six stages while making changes. James Prochaska and Carlo DiClemente developed this model in the late 1970s after studying smokers who had quit. Some did so on their own, while others required assistance (Brookes 2023).

In the first stage, precontemplation, people are not yet ready to change. The second stage, contemplation, is when people think about change but don't yet act. During the third stage, preparation, they get ready to change, and during the fourth stage, changing, they take Action. Maintaining is the fifth stage, during which people try to stick with their change for longer than six months. During the sixth and last stage, termination, the change becomes their new normal, and they have no desire to return to their old habits.

Although there are only six stages in this model, going from the early stages to the later ones could take years in some cases. If you get stuck or falter between changing and maintaining, you may never make it to termination. Between your desire for change and any challenges that may arise, you may find yourself teetering on the edge of making a commitment. Maybe the cons are greater than the pros. The longer you stay indecisive, the more you'll judge yourself and/or feel frustrated by your inaction.

I believe there's more to the contemplation stage than just thinking, *I might . . .* We may also create a running list in our heads about the challenges we may encounter. The greater the list of challenges and the greater the gap from here to there, the more fear or doubt we may have. This is when we feel stuck. Part of us wants the change and part of us is avoiding it. Instead of focusing on the difficulties that await us, we can focus on the possibilities:

- ❖ *I'm worried this will be too hard.* → *What if it's easy?*
- ❖ *I may have to give up a lot.* → *What might I gain?*
- ❖ *People might get in my way.* → *Who can help me?*

> *You have the capability to change your life all with a simple shift in perspective.*
>
> —Demi Lovato

By reframing your worrisome statements into open questions, you give yourself new possibilities and discover a new perspective or Mindset. Focusing on the benefits of making the change can give you the inspiration you need to make the commitment every day. Making a list of what you're moving toward may help you feel excited and motivated. Use that momentum to keep going, bit by bit. Just remember that you're moving toward your Best Life.

As I mentioned earlier, a strategy that can help keep you motivated is focusing on your why. The *reason* you've decided to make a change can be even more important than *what* you've decided to change. Keeping this in mind ensures that you're changing to better your life, to live your Best Life. The clearer that why, the easier it becomes to commit to and maintain your change. As the Center for The Empowerment Dynamic (n.d.b.) says, "Change occurs when people connect with an intrinsic value—something they deeply care about. When they get in touch with what matters most to them, they will invest in personal change efforts."

Some people are so eager for change that they may think making many changes is better than making just one. However, jumping into too many changes at once could spread your energy and motivation too thin. Set yourself up for success by focusing on one change at a time. Give it all you've got, put in the effort to achieve it, and create the lasting change you need to tackle the next step in the journey.

COMMITMENT, DECISIVENESS, AND CONFIDENCE

There are three important keys to achieving any goal: commitment, decisiveness, and confidence. If you're in the doubtful phase, these three feelings aren't very strong, but that doesn't mean you can't get started. It just means that you won't get far until you charge up those three engines. Then, continue to give them fuel until the goal is complete.

Commitment

> *Until one is committed, there is hesitancy, the chance to draw back, always ineffectiveness. Concerning all acts of initiative (and creation), there is one elementary truth... That the moment one definitely commits oneself, then providence moves, too. All sorts of things occur to help one that would never otherwise have occurred. A whole stream of events issues from the decision, raising in one's favour all manner of unforeseen incidents, meetings and material assistance which no man could have dreamed would have come his way.*
>
> —William H Murray, *The Scottish Himalayan Expedition*

When it comes to change, commitment isn't something that happens once. We don't decide to make a change one day, and then days, weeks, months, or even years later it just happens. Every single day is an opportunity to commit ourselves to our goal over and over again. If you're working on a particularly large goal, especially one you may have struggled to change in the past, you may need to commit to it every day for a lifetime. When you have a goal that's worth everything, when your why aligns with your values and needs, it's all the more important to find the power to act and support your need to achieve it.

Whatever your desired outcome, reflect on why you want to make the change in the first place. How will following through improve your life? What daily habits will support you in reaching and maintaining those goals? I made a commitment to having a healthy body, a strong relationship with my family, and a thriving writing and coaching practice.

Your commitments may be completely different from mine. In January, we call these New Year's resolutions. We know how those usually work out—especially if we haven't leaned into change.

How many times have you said something like, "I'm going to lose weight, organize my office, and set better boundaries?" You were determined and committed to succeed. This was important to you. You got started, but then something happened. Within a week or two of declaring any goal, you're bound to discover an obstacle in your path—something that makes you feel doubtful, frustrated, or challenged. If you take your eye off the ball, you could lose your commitment and fall back into old patterns. However, by practicing Awareness you can take back control and recommit to what you want. The faster you notice you're off track, the faster you can steer back in the right direction.

We can look at commitment in two ways: either on a sliding continuum or as an on/off switch; you're either committed or you're not. On the sliding scale, your commitment might range from faltering to rock-solid. If you notice you're less committed, you'll also notice inconsistent results. Get curious as to why you're wavering. Enlist some support to talk through the subject and gain clarity. Identify your biggest potholes, put up some warning signs, and/or patch up those potholes to make your journey smoother. When you recommit, you'll find the road more solid the next time around.

Name a goal and ask where you are on the commitment continuum:

- ❖ *I might... someday in the future.*
- ❖ *I'll try, but we all know it's not likely that I'll succeed.*
- ❖ *I'll do this one part of the plan, but not the rest.*
- ❖ *I'm 100 percent committed for a short period of time.*

❖ *I'm 100 percent committed to living in this new way forever.*

Are you thinking that the last one should be your answer? Forever is a very long time. There's a big difference between commitment to an individual task and commitment to a new way of being for your entire life. The larger and more pressing the issue, the more your old habits will come back with abandon. To live your Best Life, you need to commit to taking Action not just on day one, but every day. Every small step moves you closer. That one small change, made daily, might make such a big impact that you'll be surprised at the unexpected gains you make in the end. It might take a while, but you *will* develop a habit if you do something consistently.

I've found that if you're going to commit to something, it's best to start with one hundred percent commitment for a short period of time. Anything less than that is just exploring an option. Committing one hundred percent for a short period of time allows you to be fully engaged while also allowing your hesitant inner parts to play along with you. You can start by saying something like, "I can do anything for a short period of time," then keep adding on increasingly more time and days. Before you know it, you'll have developed a new habit, implemented a strategy, and/or acquired a new identity. Alcoholics give up booze one day at a time. Surely you can spend five dedicated minutes every day doing one new thing if the change is worthwhile. Then expand from there.

> My friend Tom's decades-long battle with getting enough sleep was something he said he wanted to change. Yet, despite his words of commitment, "I want to get more sleep," his actions did not show commitment. He kept watching his favorite

late-night shows or beginning a project at bedtime, and he was averaging only four to five hours of sleep per night. Once he asked for support in the form of accountability and tracked his sleep time, he was finally able to make progress. Sharing this progress encouraged him even more, and after a year he was averaging six hours. Upon Reflection—seeing what was working—he made a new commitment to limit TV at night, and his average sleep time jumped to seven hours. Occasionally he has a lapse, but then he recommits. Tom is leaning into change.

Exercise 9: Commit

1. Name a goal or intention you're committed to.
2. Reflect on your actions. Do they support your commitment? If yes, keep going! If not, why not? What change must you lean into?
3. Make a list of preferred actions that would better reflect a commitment.

Try these tips to boost your commitment, decisiveness, and confidence:

- ❖ Take small steps and reflect on your wins.
- ❖ Get support as you learn something new.
- ❖ Log your progress.
- ❖ Remember your why.
- ❖ Commit to figuring it out.

Decisiveness

> *All barriers fall away when you make a decision.*
> —Midge Noble, coach and author of *Gay with God*

Decisiveness, like commitment, is necessary for goal achievement. *Merriam-Webster's Dictionary* offers us a few synonyms for the word decisive: "resolute," "determined," "unmistakable," and "unquestionable." My mom's definition would've included the words "not wishy-washy!" When we're decisive, we resolve to do something very specific. We know what we want to focus on.

- ❖ Decide what you want.
- ❖ Decide to make it happen.
- ❖ Decide why this is important to you and what you're going to do if you start losing momentum or drive.

Decisiveness is very helpful for establishing "the what," but it's "the how" that often trips us up and keeps us feeling stuck. If we separate the two, we can focus on one thing at a time. Step 1 is to decide what you want. Be clear and committed. If you're not there yet, keep reading and you'll find ways to get there.

A recent client of mine had been thinking about retiring for several years but kept putting off the decision. Once they were committed and decisive that they truly were going to retire, they were able to explore options and plan what steps to take to make it happen. They had to decide on *the what*—retiring—before pursuing *the how*.

Confidence

Over the years, I've witnessed hundreds of clients transform before my very eyes. They shift from feeling stuck and discouraged about their circumstances to feeling more accomplished and confident. This shift comes from taking intentional steps toward goals that are important to them. Their eyes are brighter, and they hold their heads higher. The flow of their communication is strong and fluid rather than quiet and hesitant. They've also figured out how to manage their self-talk when life doesn't end up just as they planned. At the root of it all is a belief in themselves that didn't exist when they started. There's great value in taking baby steps, celebrating, and reflecting. That Awareness of personal growth goes a long way in building confidence.

Not every client struggles from a lack of self-confidence. However, every client I've worked with who sticks with coaching for more than a few sessions improves their self-confidence. It grows as they actively celebrate their wins—big and small, day after day, week after week, and month after month. They become more proactive and allow their Best Self to take more control of their lives.

Exercise 10: Explore Your Confidence

Taking the time to notice behavior patterns helps to unlock your ability to keep going in your desired direction. We may never be confident all the time, but we can increase our confidence if we understand what supports it. For example, I am more confident when I have practiced something many times. Ask yourself the following questions and see if you have a better understanding of your own confidence:

1. When is your confidence the highest? Why do you think that's the case?
2. When do you feel least confident? Why do you think you're less confident in those situations?
3. In what area of your life, and for what projects or issues, would you like to have more confidence?
4. What is one shift you could make toward leaning into change and raising your confidence?

As you lean into change, decide who you want to be.

Exercise 11: Lean In

If you embraced all the shifts I've suggested in these last few chapters, who would you become? Besides becoming decisive, confident, and inspired to take Action, who do you want to be? I've provided a list of suggestions, but I encourage you to make your own. You can also make a double list depicting who you no longer want to be on the left (*I no longer want to be*) and who you want to be on the right. Describe yourself as if you already are, starting with the phrase *I am*:

- *confident and happy*
- *grateful and content with my life*
- *enjoying life*
- *consciously prioritizing*
- *organized, with routines and structures that will support my life and work*
- *flexible and capable of making changes if any needs arise*
- *willing to take risks while learning from mistakes and failures*
- *mindfully setting boundaries and expectations with others*
- *actively seeking harmony in my life with no area energetically or emotionally dominating over the others*
- *focused on my outcome when stressful thoughts push me off course*

Once you have your list, begin to think about what it will take to achieve that new state of being. The next section will give you a glimpse into what might be in the way and how to overcome the obstacles.

PART TWO
Understand Yourself

> *To understand yourself is the beginning of wisdom.*
> —Jiddu Krishnamurti, *Freedom from the Known*

Part 2: Understand Yourself

Chapter 4: Nature, Nurture, and Mindfulness
Chapter 5: Thoughts
Chapter 6: Inner Self
Chapter 7: Our Inner Cast of Characters
Chapter 8: Goals, Outcomes, and Priorities

This section of the book will help you gain a greater understanding of yourself. Use these tools to learn more about your deepest and most difficult-to-achieve desired intentions, as well as what hinders you. Put on your detective hat and attempt to solve the issue of why you're stuck or why you're repeating some patterns over and over again when you don't really want to. This will help you consciously live your life more effectively, both personally and professionally. We'll focus on five areas for greater understanding: internal wiring (nature and nurture), thoughts, inner parts, Best Self, and goals.

Everyone I've encountered over my fifteen years of coaching has past actions they're proud of and others they wish they'd done better. Unfortunately, we humans tend to focus on what's going wrong. Like most coaches, this is often when I meet people who are full of frustration over not knowing how to reach a particular goal. They want something different. They're at Point A and want to be at Point B, but they aren't sure how to overcome the obstacles in their way.

No one likes to feel stuck, overwhelmed, or doubtful, especially when it comes to their priorities. The problem is that we often don't take the time to look at the issue and prioritize figuring it out. This section of the book has the tall order of helping you do just that. You'll look at yourself and begin to understand who you are at your core, what issues you struggle with, why you struggle with them, and how to find your way toward a solution.

You are wired a certain way, perhaps from birth. You have natural tendencies to act a certain way in everyday situations. Are you orderly, assertive, flexible, or creative? Are you conflict-avoidant, insecure, or controlling? Maybe you've been a certain way all your life, steering down the path you felt was laid out in front of you. Perhaps you didn't even set the path. It could've been laid out by your parents, religion, or society as a whole. Know that it's possible to change course. A small shift can take you to an entirely different destination.

Our thoughts influence everything we say and do, how we react to circumstances, and how quickly we recover from obstacles in our way. Our inner parts, the characters that feed our thoughts, may be in the forefront all the time, or they may only show up under certain circumstances. Having an Awareness of our inner parts leads to an Awareness in our thinking. Knowing what tends to trigger them gives us the control to be our Best Self. While you may have a Judge, Procrastinator, Perfectionist, or other parts within you, give yourself time to learn about each one and how they operate.

You have the capacity to be your Best Self, which helps you deal with everything from relationships and stress to daily chores, leadership issues, running a business, and so on. Being decisive in setting priorities helps you choose the areas you want to focus on. This helps you stay committed all the way through to Completion. Selecting your goals is a very personal thing, and rightly so. To get you to the final destination you desire, we'll dive into the world of goal-directed change and learn how to set goals that address what you want.

CHAPTER 4
NATURE, NURTURE, AND MINDFULNESS

> *Each and every one of us is who we are because of both nature and nurture. The good news is that, through mindfulness, we can continue to nurture ourselves and change who we ultimately become.*
>
> —Monica Leggett

Nature, Nurture, and Mindfulness

- Nature
- Nurture
- Mindfulness
- Acceptance, Compromise, and Adaptation

We are the recipients of many things beyond our control. Nature is what we're born with: our genetics, personality, and physical appearance. Nurture is what influences us - once we're born: our environment, relationships, and experiences. Mindfulness allows us to take what life has given us (nature and nurture), and mold it into what we want. I've included this chapter to help you explore why you are the way you are—why you think and act the way you do. Then, with new Awareness and skills, you'll be more at choice in how to respond in future situations.

Of all our organs, the brain is the most important for supporting us through making changes. With it, we can learn new concepts, identify challenges, think up solutions, convince ourselves to take Action, commit to change, and work through our plan until Completion. Our thoughts stem from both our innate wiring as well as our life experiences. Though we can't be mechanically rewired like a car engine if we want better performance, we can use certain strategies to redirect our thoughts and actions. By repeatedly responding differently to an event, we mentally rewire (change) how we think—even while something like our basic traits or personality stays the same. The key is to understand ourselves before we can apply mindfulness. Let's start with nature.

NATURE

The brain is a network of nerves that carry electrical impulses, causing the body to complete certain functions in an orderly manner. Signals pass from one nerve cell to another. This link of cells is called a **neural pathway**. The more frequently a pathway is used, the stronger it becomes and the faster an impulse will travel, making it more likely we will react the same way each time to the same stimulus. We were born with a certain order to our neural pathways—our nature or operating system.

Neural pathways allow our bodies to function without thinking. Our hearts beat, our lungs breathe, and our bodies move in whatever direction we wish. Beyond keeping our primary organs functioning, neural pathways develop for other purposes as we repeat behaviors over and over again. Once the neural pathways are well-developed, an activity becomes an automatic, conditioned response or routine, such as getting ready for bed. We don't think, *This is how to brush my teeth*, we just do it.

Though there are helpful automatic responses, such as moving out of the road when a car is coming, we can develop learned responses. Our instincts to react to situations or stimuli eventually become the habits that make up a good part of our day. Think of the number of times and ways your automatic path takes you where you don't want to go. You've developed habits without even realizing it!

- ❖ I sit down at night to watch TV. → I have the urge to eat. → I go get something to eat.
- ❖ The phone pings that I have an incoming message. → I pick up my phone right away.
- ❖ I see a pile of papers to sort. → I feel like it's too much right now. → I do something else, anything else.
- ❖ I hear a complaint from a coworker. → I judge them. → I tune them out or chime in.
- ❖ My alarm goes off in the morning. → I decide I don't want to get up. → I hit the snooze button, go back to sleep, and suffer the consequences.

> **Certain neural pathways in your brain may be the roads less traveled, while others are the superhighways you take all the time.**

Personality

> *Personality refers to the enduring characteristics and behavior that comprise a person's unique adjustment to life, including major traits, interests, drives, values, self-concept, abilities, and emotional patterns.*
>
> —American Psychological Association

Our internal wiring influences our personality traits. Between the 1950s and the 1980s, a series of research teams evaluated them all in an effort to create a list of the basic factors of personality. By the 1980s, Paul Costa and Robert R. McCrae of the National Institutes of Health confirmed five specific traits that we develop from a very young age and that are consistent throughout our lifetime, now known as "the Big Five" (Kelland n.d.). Each exists on a continuum of low to high prevalence and can be measured through testing. The Big Five personality traits are as follows:

1. Openness—measures creativity and imagination versus more traditional thinking
2. Conscientiousness—measures organization, attention to detail, and self-discipline
3. Extraversion—measures someone's outgoing, energetic, and social nature
4. Agreeableness—measures how cooperative someone is, possibly desiring to put someone else's needs before their own
5. Neuroticism—measures someone's sensitivity and tendency to lean into anxiety, depression, and negative feelings

Exercise 12: Who Have You Always Been?

Think back to your childhood. What patterns and behaviors have been around your whole life?

1. Were you outgoing or shy?
2. Were you inquisitive, needing to find out more, or did you take things at face value?
3. Were you an assertive leader or more of a follower who went with the flow?
4. What else stands out about who you were as a child? Are you still that way now?

Personality Types

Figuring out our personality types can be just for fun, or it can be to open the door to understanding our innate wiring. As Kelland (n.d.) notes, "Trait theorists have repeatedly shown that traits are highly resistant to change once adulthood has been reached." Isn't it better to know what parts of us are resistant to change (those that are embedded in our wiring) so that we can learn how to use them and shed light on areas of potential growth?

There are many assessment options to evaluate our personality types. My favorite assessment, and the one I'm certified to use with all my clients, is **PeopleMap™**. It was developed by Michael Lillibridge and Andrew Mathis, two PhD holders and research psychologists who wanted a tool that was quick to assess and easy to understand. Their main premise was that if we can understand ourselves and others better, we can learn to speak their language and improve our communication skills. I've had great success using the tool with individuals, couples, and teams.

The four personality types in the PeopleMap assessment are Leader, People, Task, and Free Spirit (Lillibridge 1998). Each of the four types are within us, just at different levels. Understanding our personal PeopleMap, including how strong each type is and in what order, gives us a glimpse into our wiring and reveals our strengths and motivators, our likely communication styles, and more.

Task and Free Spirit are opposite types, as are Leader and People. If you imagine four managers at a table, each assigned to solve a problem, they would each have their own focus. You might see these four approaches: The Task type uses logic and past wins to find their answers, and they're slower paced because they want to get things right. The Free Spirit type thinks fast and goes with their instincts to solve problems in unconventional ways. The Leader type is named that for a reason—they're upfront, results-oriented, decisive, and fast-paced. People types want to lead by consensus, ensuring everyone is heard and happy with the results, so they take their time to be able to reach consensus.

When personality types differ, it takes skills in listening, Acceptance, and compromise to find solutions. These are all learned skills, not part of our innate wiring. So let's move on to explore how our environment and experiences—our nurturing—continues to shape us.

Nurture

While each personality type has its own key strengths, they each have potential vulnerabilities as well. This is where our nature combines with our nurturing to influence who we become. As Dr. Lillibridge explained it to me, each personality type has core strengths and needs, and if they're left unchecked, a need can become an **Achilles heel**: a weakness or vulnerability.

For example, a People type is typically a great communicator and motivated to help people, but they also seek harmony and are reinforced by approval. Throughout their life, they learned what made their parents, teachers, and coworkers happy and what made them upset. Their nifty little brain wanted harmony and approval so much that it caused a tendency to become a people-pleaser and conflict avoider—at their own expense. Similarly, a Leader type might be motivated by achieving results, but they might also micromanage, become intolerably impatient, or be a workaholic.

When we aren't practicing mindfulness, our unmet core needs can lead to our Achilles heels. I offer the following exercise as an opportunity to become familiar with your Achilles heels, and in chapter 6 we'll explore them further.

Exercise 13: Identify Your Achilles Heels

1. What need do you have that can go too far and become an Achilles heel? For example, independence, acceptance, control, belonging, or perfection.
2. Name your trait in terms of both its need and Achilles heel. For example, Harmonizer / Pleaser and Detail-Oriented / Perfectionist.
3. How does your Achilles heel affect your personal and professional life?
4. What other need has led to an Achilles heel? (Repeat steps 2 and 3.)
5. How would you like to describe yourself in the future if you were to consciously work to diminish your Achilles heels? For instance, "My husband is becoming more flexible, and I am becoming more focused."

> *I'm going to stop trying to be perfect ...*
> *and trust that the Universe has me in its hands.*
>
> —Molly Sargent, Mindfulness Practitioner

Think about how our lives have influenced who we are today. Each of us is molded by the nurturing we receive as well as our circumstances, the people around us, and the wins, failures, and traumas we've experienced. These factors may have caused us to become more cautious or adventurous, more miserly or reckless, more timid or outspoken.

Our nurturing goes one step further: Intentionally or unintentionally, the people in our lives, especially when we're young, model how to act and how to be. Words and actions from influential adults and childhood bullies can become the thoughts in our heads that encourage or discourage us for the rest of our lives. Our environment and experiences don't necessarily rewire us or change our personality per se, but they mold our beliefs and values, which eventually become our default ways of life. When we take the time to explore our thoughts and actions, we begin to see what operating system is at the driver's seat and can choose to either accept and embrace that modeling or reject and replace it.

I don't presume that my book can help you heal from any trauma you've gone through. I can only offer a lens through which to see what has shaped the way you think now in an effort to help you become more aware and lean into change.

Beliefs, Values, and Habits

We can likely all agree that our upbringing and experiences affect who we are. During our younger years, we adopt many beliefs and values that come from the people and cultures that surround us. As our experiences expand, so do our beliefs and values. In turn, these go on to influence our thoughts, feelings, and actions, as well as the results we're able to achieve. Let's explore what informs our beliefs, values, and eventually our habits so that we can see opportunities to improve our lives. You may find that what seemed true as a child is now very outdated!

Beliefs

As children, we have very little control over our lives, yet it's during childhood that the foundations for our belief systems are built. Our ingrained beliefs, especially those seeded in our childhood, can be very hard to uproot. Those beliefs help form the thoughts that support our default actions. I know people in their seventies and eighties who are still working through issues of self-worth and scarcity that they've had all their lives due to their upbringing.

We can create just as many beliefs from a lack of knowledge or experience as we do from knowing all about something or experiencing it firsthand. For instance, distorted beliefs may develop as a result of not getting certain types of attention. Not receiving enough love, Acceptance, acknowledgment, or affirmation could cause someone to become over-obliging and accepting of others. Without the balance of setting boundaries and expectations, that person could end up supporting the behavior of a high-chair tyrant who grows into a self-centered adult.

We see some beliefs that we develop over our lifetime as values-based rules to live by or social norms. They may be very true to the believer while absolutely not true for those who surround them. Racial, gender, or any other bias is predominantly based on cultural beliefs. They may even be based on beliefs held by past generations and have been born out of defunct social norms or societal traumas. My parents, for example, grew up in the 1930s during the Great Depression. As a result, we lived with a sense of scarcity; we were careful with money, food, and our belongings. We didn't expect many material things, and we certainly didn't waste anything! I was born over twenty years after their experiences, yet I still share some of their beliefs from that time. Parents can pass down perseverance and pride, but they can also pass down bias and trauma.

While some people hold firm to the beliefs of their parent's generation, others rebel against what they believe are outdated ways of thinking. The decades of the 1960s and 1970s are a great example. The adults had a lot of resistance to their children spreading their wings, seemingly going against all the beliefs and ideals they had in mind for them. I was the seventh of ten kids, and many of the rules for my older siblings were softened by the time I graduated from high school. Here are a few strong beliefs I was exposed to during my youth:

- ❖ Girls and boys should be raised and encouraged differently.
- ❖ Everyone should go away to a four-year college (a progressive belief encouraged by my grandfather).
- ❖ Everyone must get a job in high school to help pay for college.

We don't have to follow the beliefs of prior generations. We may be exposed to new beliefs (or adopt our own) and have the choice of which beliefs to follow. My siblings held onto some of our family's beliefs, but they also let go of some that no longer served them, despite resistance from family and society. For instance, in 1967, my sister Katherine wanted to be an accountant like my father. He told her, "Business is no place for a lady. No daughter of mine will get a job in the business world! You should get a job as a teacher and be home with your kids in the summer." She ended up graduating with a degree in Spanish and even got her master's degree. Years later, believing she could better provide for her family, she went back to school to earn her MBA and eventually became the CFO of a bank. Her career in business at a time when few women were in the field meant she was the lone woman in many board meetings. Ultimately, in many ways, she was much more successful than my father.

My sister Grace started a PhD in chemistry in the mid-1970s. After experiencing two years of gender bias at her graduate school in the Midwest, she left with a master's degree. For the rest of her career, Grace worked to develop her own leadership skills and break down barriers. As a coach, she developed a training program in diversity, equity, and inclusion. Ultimately, Grace didn't let the limiting beliefs of our family or society hold her back from living the life she wanted, providing countless others with the support to do the same.

My sister Charlotte, just four years younger than Grace, served in the Peace Corps teaching chemistry in a village in Africa that had no running water. Afterward, she completed a PhD in chemistry at MIT. When I asked Charlotte what was different for her, she said that although her experience at the Northeast liberal school wasn't completely free of gender bias, it was very different from Grace's. She was very passionate about her career path and didn't let discrimination get to her. She has since had a thirty-year career as a chemistry teacher, influencing thousands of students as an intelligent female role model.

As for my husband and I, we wanted to instill the messages that education is essential, work has value, and being proactive determines your destination. We set out to raise competent, self-sufficient adults and to model the values and beliefs that we felt were important. They learned how to do every chore and were expected to pick up after themselves. Everyone learned how to pitch in because we were a team. By the time they were fifteen, our kids were doing their own laundry, deciding how to spend their clothing allowance, and finding ways to earn money for incidentals and college. We continued the same expectation of a college education and helped them pay for it (unlike my parents), but they also had jobs, scholarships, loans, or all three.

I'm so proud of what I observe in my children! (Steve and I must've done something right.) I watch them intentionally teaching and modeling kindness, charity, and love to their children. My children want their children to grow up as mentally and physically healthy, capable human beings who contribute to society.

Exercise 14: Explore Your Beliefs

As Rogers and Hammerstein so brilliantly wrote about in their song "You've Got to Be Carefully Taught," we all had many messages drummed in our "dear little ear" as a child. Sometimes we were taught intentionally, but other times we learned through observation and experience. Did you receive love, Acceptance, and empathy, or were you fed judgment, blame, distrust, and apathy? Were you discouraged from taking risks by helicopter parents, or were you thrown into uncomfortable situations and encouraged to bravely give them a try? Did you grow up feeling safe, cared for, and with a sense of belonging, or were you bullied and teased by classmates, perhaps even family members?

What are some of your deep-seated beliefs, and where do you think they come from?

- ❖ Modeling observed in childhood
- ❖ Family and/or friends
- ❖ Coworkers and bosses
- ❖ Religious influences
- ❖ Life itself

What beliefs would you intentionally like to model or pass down to your children or others you love?

Values

Ethics Unwrapped (n.d.) of the University of Texas defines values as, "Individual beliefs that motivate people to act one way or another. They serve as a guide for human behavior." A short list of values might include integrity, truth, respect, fairness, and accomplishment. Your strongest values influence your thoughts about accomplishments, career, family, connections, personal well-being, spirituality, financial health, surroundings, and adventure.

Values are very personal. When it comes to a career, one person may value making money while another person values making a difference. They don't have to be mutually exclusive, but they're both important if the person owns a business and is trying to make an income instead of having a perpetual hobby.

If we aren't living our values, or if our values are in conflict with each other, it can cause internal strife. One of my clients noticed that they weren't making enough money because they were putting everyone else's needs ahead of their own: *Sure, I'll throw in one more service, keep my rates low, and even buy things for you as my treat.* There's an epidemic of people who don't charge what their skills, experience, and time are worth. They need to stand their ground and set boundaries instead of avoiding discomfort and potential rejection.

Exercise 15: Consider Your Values

To get in touch with your values, think about the qualities that give your life meaning. Think back to times when you have the strongest memories, then answer these questions:

1. What gets you excited?
2. When do you thrive and prosper?
3. What upsets you?

Your top values may be those you feel have been most important in your life so far or what you want to have more of in your Best Life.

Another way to discover your values is to examine a current struggle in your life. List five values related to it. For example, you may be disagreeing with a friend or family member about something they've been saying or doing. What values are being overlooked or violated? Fairness, loyalty, and respect are a few that may come to mind. Asking yourself these questions can lead you to a deeper understanding of what you value when it comes to relationships. One of the most difficult self-awareness exercises I ever experienced was trying to whittle down my values to the top five. So to help you do the same, I've provided a long list of values at MonicaLeggett.com that you can refer to when making your top-ten list.

Habits

> *A habit is a behavior that has been repeated enough times to become automatic.*
>
> —James Clear, *Atomic Habits*

Habits typically follow a cue or a trigger, like eating or drinking after stressful events. They're formed on an unconscious level. Our habits evolved over time as we laid down strong neural pathways, but they didn't start out as habits. Most people have habits around morning and evening hygiene, meals, cleaning, organization, spirituality, responding to conflict, and more. You might even have a habit of responding with a resounding NO anytime you're asked to try something new and before you've even thought about it.

Some habits begin in our childhood, and others develop over our lifetime. Some are great habits, and others become limiting obstacles. When we desire large outcomes such as good health, an organized home, a successful business, and a happy family, we may start by establishing a routine—doing things intentionally and repeatedly. Then we hope that over time it will become a habit. Good habits are intentionally created with our goals in mind. However, some habits begin randomly and grow unconsciously, such as eating snacks when watching TV or biting your nails when nervous.

It would be wonderful if our lives were filled with good habits that support everything we want in our Best Life, but it's not that simple. Not only do we develop derailing habits in areas where we aren't mindful of our actions, but we also have habit gaps. These are places where habits would be beneficial but either we haven't taken the time to figure them out or we feel resistant to the effort and change it might create.

Why do we resist developing new habits that we know we want? I can think of many people who wish they had certain good habits, including going to bed earlier, spending more time reading or journaling, or pausing before they jump into a situation. There are tons of entrepreneurs who wish they regularly posted on social media or turned a spontaneous photo into an Instagram post. Other people might wish they spent less time on social media, less time watching TV, and less time mindlessly eating at night. Their ideal habit might be giving something up or starting something new to make a change for the better.

Routines are repeated behaviors, without a particular trigger, that ultimately become natural to us, such as doing similar things each morning or at bedtime. For instance, Melissa works part-time from home and has gotten into a routine that balances her work and life. In the morning she checks her work phone to get a sense of what she might be dealing with that day. If there are no emergencies, she does what she wants until 9 a.m. Depending on her mood, she might take a walk, do yoga, or clean the kitchen. When she starts work at 9 a.m., she feels ready to face the day—with gas in her tank, so to speak.

One day, Steve and I saw our twenty-year-old nephew, Phil (who we know as an artist, not an athlete), go out for a run. He came back about twenty minutes later, tired but exhilarated. Several times a week Phil would run, each time a little bit further, and each time coming back a little less winded. Steve regularly worked out with weights, but he had never tried running. Being a competitive guy, he thought it looked like a good addition to his workout routine.

Steve's first attempt was difficult, but three times a week after lifting weights he'd go for a run. One mile turned to two and then three. Within six months, Steve was running eight miles three days a week. Without realizing it, he was taking advantage of a great way to add new habits to his routine. **Habit stacking**, a term coined by S. J. Scott, is when you add one new habit to an already existing habit (Scott 2017).

As Steve formed this new habit, his identity changed—he became a runner. With the Mindset, *I can do it,* he made a commitment, and that turned into a habit: working out with weights and running eight miles three times a week. When traveling he'd check out the gym facilities and look for good routes to run in the area. I've seen Steve run along the Nile in Egypt, on trails in Switzerland, and near the beach in Hawaii.

Steve isn't happy if he has to skip his workouts. His limiting beliefs still creep in sometimes: *I have to work out three times a week. It's not worth doing if I can't do my full workout. I'll lose strength if I miss a workout.* Thankfully, these limiting beliefs show up less often now than they did at the beginning. Steve has also given himself some slack, taken days off if he pulls a muscle, and taken it easy if he has done a big house project. Now Steve has a new belief: *It's okay to be flexible.*

Exercise 16: Recognize Your Habits

Think about your own habits. Are there any you proudly created? Are there some you'd like to begin or eliminate? Do you have tendencies (not quite habits) that seem to get in the way of your happiness? How have your beliefs and habits influenced your reactions to everyday issues? Here are a few questions you can ask yourself to gain clarity about your habits:

1. What do I do habitually and then regret later?
2. Do I want to address something about what I'm doing or not doing?
3. Is there a habit I'd like to start or end?
4. What is the first step I can take?

Mindfulness

> *The goal of mindfulness is to wake up to the inner workings of our mental, emotional, and physical processes.*
>
> —Mindful.org

One of the best tools for strengthening the specific neural pathways that we believe will benefit our Best Self the most is mindfulness: a practice of being present in the moment, noticing our thoughts, and being intentional with our actions. Many people react without thinking, allowing their default wiring or habits to control their results. Mindfulness allows us to stop before we get carried away, to think beyond this moment to how the choice we make now will impact the Best Life that we're trying to create.

Forging Paths and Blazing Trails

> *If you don't like the road you're walking, start paving another one.*
>
> —Dolly Parton

Imagine this: You live in the middle of the forest, and the only paved roads are the same ones you always travel. They go to the same places and give you the same experiences and results you've always had. One day on a walk, you notice a cottage in the distance, but there's no way to get to it. You decide to forge a new path, cutting the trail as you go, but as it gets more difficult you give up. On the one hand, the hard work and mud you get stuck in aren't worth it, yet on the other hand, you're still intrigued by reaching the cottage and the possibilities it may hold.

The next day, you're once again back to clearing the path. As you get closer to the cottage, you notice someone standing near it, perhaps a neighbor you've never met. Now you're even more determined to reach the cottage to introduce yourself. You stop when it gets dark each day, then resume work the next morning. With determination and commitment, you finally reach the cottage and are greeted by a wonderful person with a soothing voice and kind manner. The two of you discuss how you could be in the world—happy, content, and grateful to be alive. Every visit makes your newly blazed trail wider and easier to follow, increasing your confidence and leading you to make plans for your future.

The person in the cottage represents your Best Self, with confident thoughts and a big vision for the future. The path you've created represents the new choices you make—new habits that over time create deeply developed neural pathways. These will take you from stimulus to response in a much quicker way and with less thought, distraction, and effort. Managing those incidental situations will become second nature. Habits can be literal, such as brushing your teeth when you get up in the morning, or they can be a different kind of habit, a deep, knowing habit, such as these:

- ❖ Knowing to pause, breathe, and calm yourself in stressful moments
- ❖ Knowing when enough is good enough because perfection isn't real
- ❖ Knowing that you have what it takes to handle life's challenges

Practicing your new choices and deciding what to do helps you grow healthy habits, beliefs, and thoughts. With regular practice, they stay steady and readily available to you. However, if you haven't traveled that path for a while, the obstacles will grow back, and your well-tended path will become hidden from view. For instance, you might begin a morning meditation routine but then keep forgetting to do it. Instead of getting on with your day as usual, you need to add a pause when you wake up, then breathe and set your intention. Give yourself a minute to consciously take that dirt path option to help pave it into a superhighway.

> **If you add a pause between any event or thought and the Action you take in response to it, you allow yourself to respond intentionally—mindfully.**

Habits aren't the only time we react automatically. When we're caught in a difficult situation, we may find ourselves getting upset rather quickly. Some call this being "triggered" or "hijacked." Our mind begins to fill with **limiting beliefs**: thoughts about ourselves or others that limit the belief in our ability to move forward or accomplish a task. For example, when I get stuck trying to solve a problem, a limiting belief might be, *I'll never figure this out.* If I believe that thought, it may cause an automatic, reactive response (fight/flight/freeze/or appease).

After some Awareness of how we've reacted in the past, we might realize that we're following the same patterns that got us stuck, frustrated, or anxious in the first place. Mindfulness can help us break that pattern and choose a new response. If I pause long enough to challenge my limiting belief, I can think, *I will figure this out.* Each time I choose that new path, I develop a stronger neural pathway toward the new response.

Mindfulness can help you break automatic responses and strengthen your desired neural pathways.

The study of neuroscience teaches us many things, including the bias our brain has toward negative thinking—finding fault and worrying about the past or the future (Vaish, Grossman, and Woodward 2008). Humans are wired to protect themselves. We want to stay safe and are wary of anything that can shake up the status quo. It's like our brains have Velcro for the bad and Teflon for the good. We focus more on the things that can and do go wrong instead of appreciating the things that can and do go well. As we do this over and over, we reinforce the neural pathways—the superhighways of our habits, default actions, and responses—that make up our personalities. "But there is an alternative to fueling our fears and limiting our self-awareness" (Zajonc

2022, 7). That alternative is mindfulness. If we want to make changes, we need to think about how we reinforce our wiring. We need to change how we act and react, then repeat those new behaviors over time to reinforce our new way of being.

Neuroscience-based research has proven over the years that the brain is not "fixed" as was previously assumed but is able to change. This is commonly called neuroplasticity: "the ability of the nervous system to change its activity in response to intrinsic or extrinsic stimuli by reorganizing its structure, functions, or connections" (Mateos-Aparicio and Rodriguez-Moreno 2019). Don't let the science scare you. What it means is that you can change your brain wiring for the better!

What would it take to change your automatic responses? Unfortunately, there isn't an app on your smartphone to change you in an instant. Real change requires effort. You need Awareness, presence, and decisiveness that you want to react differently, which means choosing a new path instead of deferring to the one you always travel. The more you practice training your thinking and choosing the path you want to follow, the stronger and deeper the neural pathways that support your Best Life will become. Take a look at the following four diagrams:

Developing New Neural Pathways with Mindfulness:
From L to R, The default response is well paved with just a hint of an alternative option; widening that new path; both options seem accessible; over time the stronger neural pathway is developed.

The change illustrated in this series of diagrams takes time. The initial picture shows a well-developed pattern of responding in one particular way, but there is a hint of a new way to respond. It's the dirt path that is rarely traveled. In each successive diagram, the new way to respond gets stronger and stronger until it becomes the new default way of responding. You cannot easily change your inborn personality traits, but you can rewire some of your default habits and automatic responses. This takes mindfulness and intentionality.

One simple practice that can develop beneficial neural pathways is the practice of gratitude, or noticing what's going well. The more you notice the positive, the less often you'll focus on what's wrong with the world. Your brain will begin to automatically look for what's good rather than what's bad, scary, or "impossible." This is why I start all my coaching sessions with "Wins for the week."

To practice gratitude, begin with just two minutes per day, saying or writing about people, situations, and things to be grateful for. You can also share them with others on a regular basis: "I'm so grateful you helped me yesterday. I really appreciate it." I guarantee that if you do this exercise daily for a month or two, you'll start to see a shift in your thinking and become Velcro for the good.

Acceptance, Compromise, and Adaptation

As humans we're a unique species, but we're also unique from one person to another. Our strengths and idiosyncrasies may complement or assist our work with others, or they may create perpetual battles. However, no one person is right or wrong; they're just different. The most effective families and teams have learned to accept and value each other for the varied strengths each person brings. Instead of judging each other or avoiding conversations to talk about your differences, I encourage you to explore the situation and find ways to accept, compromise, and adapt, thereby allowing you to experience a life of ease alongside someone you might otherwise be at odds with. What are you willing to do for the sake of your relationships?

Acceptance, compromise, and adaptation are all helpful strategies I've used with my husband for the sake of our marriage. Steve and I have many opposite traits, but we're still on the same page about the values we live by and our shared goals. Passing judgment on one another doesn't allow us to live harmoniously. Instead of engaging in a battle of wills over our differences, we adopted strategies that work for us. He is left-handed, for example, while I am right-handed. If we sit next to each other at a meal, I sit to his right, otherwise we bump elbows the entire meal. I don't judge him for being left-handed, and he doesn't judge me for being right-handed. So why would we judge each other over other ways we're wired differently? He's an introvert and likes to go home early, but I prefer to squeeze the most joy out of every party (and help the hostess clean up), so I'm often one of the last to leave. Instead of arguing about when to head home, we often take two cars.

Steve and I have learned to compromise for the sake of our forty-three-year marriage, mainly because we love one another, but also because we accept each other—differences and all. We want to be our Best Selves living our Best Lives together. We accept that our default preferences are still there and make an effort to find ways to adapt and change. This allows us to grow together, not apart.

Whether your opposite is a romantic partner or a business partner, this strategy can be a wonderful tool in all aspects of your life. Learn to speak each other's language, understand each other, and accept each other. Find what you have in common. Your drama will be replaced with curiosity and authentic conversations, which will lead to growth and connection instead of stubborn opposition.

Notice your differences, don't judge them, and see how you can help one another succeed. Become a leader by showing others how to embrace differences and communicate more effectively. This can result in positive shifts in families, teams, and organizations. All this insight and understanding is the door to intentional proactive change.

Exercise 17: Practice Mindfulness

1. Name a path you'd like to redirect—perhaps a habit or reactive response that gets in your way or an Achilles heel you'd like to change.

2. Create a thirty-day tracking sheet to document any time that habit or reaction takes place.

    → What were the circumstances prior to the result?

    → What would you prefer to do instead?

3. Add a five-minute mindfulness session each day when you imagine yourself responding in your preferred way. For example, if someone appears to be judging you, take it as a helpful observation and an opportunity to learn. If you're avoiding a necessary task, choose to set a timer for five minutes and take some small Action toward your desired result.

CHAPTER 5
THOUGHTS

> *The greatest discovery of all time is that a person can change [their] future by merely changing [their] attitude.*
>
> —Oprah Winfrey

- ➢ Limiting Beliefs
- ➢ Dial Up, Dial Down
- ➢ Fear
- ➢ Thoughts. Feelings. Actions. Results.
- ➢ Noticing Your Mindset

Slow down, tune into your thoughts, and examine them. You might be surprised by how often you judge yourself or others, talk yourself out of things, and focus on a distorted version of reality. Consider journaling your thoughts for a few days. You'd be amazed by what you're saying to yourself! Once you realize what's going on, you can shift to a more positive stream of motivating thoughts.

Thoughts are the keys to our success. When we live our lives on autopilot, we don't even tune into our thoughts. Instead of being mindful, we mindlessly go about our days without setting intentions. We continue doing the same things, reacting the same ways, and possibly making the same mistakes over and over again, yet we rarely—if ever—explore our thoughts as to why. Thoughts have the power to help us achieve our goals, find success, and create our Best Life.

When living on autopilot, we believe our thoughts and act on them. We forget that thoughts are not necessarily facts. Thoughts may be true, but they may also be false. Our thoughts are an internal interpretation of what's going on around us based on our beliefs, values, and experiences.

> *Your inner thoughts aren't truly hidden.*
> *Their essence reflects in your energy.*
> *Energy speaks what you don't.*
>
> —Drishti Bablani, philanthropist and author

Even though we think no one can see the inner workings of our minds, we still give off the energy of the types of thoughts we're having. Surely you've been in a bad mood and everyone around you knew it. Your energy was revealing itself in your actions. Negative thoughts can make us feel like we can't do, say, or live a certain way. They may be about ourselves, the world, or life in general. While negative thoughts can drain our energy, positive thoughts can give us the fuel to keep going, even in the face of a challenge.

Thoughts About Challenges

Everyone experiences challenges. No matter how put together someone seems, they're always struggling with something. It's how they respond to the issue that matters. If we backtrack decisions we make by second-guessing ourselves, we'll start going in reverse. If we find ourselves focusing on our struggles and feeling stuck and doubtful, we'll stay in neutral. If we reframe our thoughts and look forward, we'll move into drive and take Action.

It's our thoughts that determine what gear we're in.

Our thoughts can work against us, or they can drive us to be decisive, take Action, reach Completion, and grow from the experience. The higher the level of Awareness of our thoughts that we gain, the more we can learn about ourselves and the challenges we face. Our ability to dial down the voice of our sabotaging inner parts will become easier while turning the dial up on our clear-minded, focused, decisive parts. We'll discuss inner parts more in the next chapter, but first a note about challenges.

You might think of challenges as issues, struggles, hurdles, or problems to solve. I like to think of challenges as temporary obstacles as well as opportunities. That way, I'm already imagining that I'll get beyond them and learn from the experience. To effectively get unstuck and be able to take Action, we need to delve a little deeper into the ways we interpret situations and decide whether they're a problem or an opportunity.

A recent article in the *New York Times* revealed the power of thought, giving examples of how people pursued new careers during the pandemic when their previous jobs were shut down (Friedman and Goldberg 2022). In each case, the person was able to shift their thinking from what was wrong to what was possible—a type of reframing. Turning challenges into opportunities led them to completely different careers. Whether they're forced upon us or we're facing them to improve our everyday lives, life hands us challenges. Our success depends on how we deal with those challenges, as the article proves. People changed their lives and livelihoods for the better during a pandemic that threatened their lives. Bravo!

Thoughts Lead to Feelings

Throughout this book, I've named inner parts, some of which may chime in and cause feelings that sabotage our actions. I've mentioned the Judge, Avoider, and Pleaser, just to name a few. Our parts play a role in our thoughts, feelings, and actions. When we understand our thoughts, we begin to see what inner part has scripted them, which gives us the opportunity to mold our outcomes as we move forward.

We all have inner parts whose limiting beliefs trip us up. It's been my experience that any time I become aware of an important outcome I want, part of me speaks up and identifies every reason I won't be able to do it:

- Organize. *That will take too much time, and I'm terrible at purging things I don't need.*
- Retire, have a difficult conversation, or get a different job. *This isn't the right time.*
- Pick one project to focus on. *They're all important; I have to do them all.*

Limiting Beliefs

We are the sum of our experiences, and we use those experiences and beliefs to make decisions. However, sometimes we're presented with an issue we have little or no positive experience dealing with. When this happens, we may make assumptions. Our minds try to fill in the blanks and create a story we believe to be true. Here are a few examples from actual clients over the years:

- A woman gives birth to a child with special needs. She believes that she must now give up all her goals and aspirations to care for her child.
- An adult is suddenly faced with caring for their elderly parent(s). They believe they must take control of all aspects of care and are sure this will ruin their lives.
- A couple is planning their wedding. They believe they need to please everyone.

Whenever we have a limiting thought about ourselves or others that can't be proven to be true, that's a limiting belief. For example, the thoughts *Girls can't major in business* and *I'll never get it done* are confining thoughts that hold us back from reaching our goals instead of pushing us forward. They keep the possibilities in our world smaller and our options limited. However, not all limiting beliefs stop us from taking Action; sometimes they cause us to do the exact opposite. *It needs to be perfect* is a thought that can push us to exhaustion at the expense of our health, our relationships, and our peace of mind.

I was very excited about going to college. I knew I'd be a good student who could handle living away from home. However, my excitement fizzled out when it came to one issue: paying for school myself. *Go away to college + Pay for it myself + I don't have a way to raise the money = I can't do this!* Lacking confidence and having limiting beliefs impacted my thought process and caused me to procrastinate, delaying my taking the necessary steps to apply. My inner Judge thought I didn't have what it would take to persevere and raise the funds.

With deadlines looming, I accepted support from my sister and a friend. I went to a local bank and filled out the paperwork to apply for a loan. I was awarded a few small scholarships plus a bank loan. In the end, it all worked out—I was going away to college. With support, I was able to talk myself through the challenge and seek solutions.

Challenge Those Thoughts!

Procrastination, based on a number of limiting beliefs, has been a theme all my life. Something to do? *It can wait.* It's important! *I'll get to it later.* The pattern had to repeat itself many times and over decades for me to realize how crippling of a habit it was. I had an automatic response to delay any time I was unsure. Some lessons are like that—we need to learn them over and over.

Another pattern I noticed was my assumption about time. I used to think that I didn't have enough time to do things. As it turns out, I wasn't being proactive and creating a plan to make the most of the time I did have. One day, I was tired of telling myself I didn't have time. There were a few ingredients I needed from the grocery store to cook dinner. If I had waited until after my 4 p.m. meeting, I would've ended up eating dinner very late. So I decided to challenge myself. Instead of waiting, I went to the store and was back in less than thirty minutes. I had plenty of time and disproved my limiting belief. Moving forward, I could think back to that scenario and remember my success. Whenever I heard that voice in my head say, *You don't have time to do that*, I responded, *Oh yes I do! Even if I only get started, it's better than not starting at all.*

Next time you feel yourself falling for a limiting belief, challenge yourself to disprove it. Reveal the lie! Once you do, you'll have more power to help push yourself toward the goals you set for living your Best Life.

Recognizing Limiting Beliefs

Limiting beliefs come in different forms, but they often include all-or-nothing thinking, extreme words, and comparisons. They may use the words "always" or "never," "impossible" and "can't," "should" or "shouldn't," and "must" or "mustn't." These thoughts may have been based on limiting beliefs, an assumption, or a worst-case scenario. The more we think them, the more we believe they're true. When you make a statement, in your mind or out loud, notice the way your body feels:

- ❖ *I'll never have time to do that.*
- ❖ *I can't learn all this new technology!*
- ❖ *It has to be this way.*

Do you have a bad feeling in the pit of your stomach? Does the thought make you anxious, sad, or small? Ask yourself if it's really true or just a limiting belief.

Can a true statement also be limiting? You may think, *I don't have time*, but perhaps the truth is actually *I don't have time right now*. Limiting belief statements will always turn the dial down, narrowing your focus and blocking out the world of possibilities before you. Even if they push you to work hard, it isn't sustainable. Acting from a decisive place, not out of fear, is what will help you grow into your Best Self.

What we spend time thinking about has a huge impact on which neural pathways we're developing into superhighways. If we focus on limiting beliefs and the possibility of stressful obstacles, we'll become hesitant to strive for what we want. Instead, we can become resilient by quickly choosing to get back on the path to our Best Self. With mindfulness, we can shift our Mindsets whenever we're ready and willing to choose a new path.

Exercise 18: Identify Your Limiting Beliefs

1. Name some of your typical limiting beliefs around the life you live, the outcomes you want, or the steps you might need to take to achieve them. When you're experiencing limiting beliefs, what are your thoughts focused on?

   → Are you ruminating over problems or looking for solutions?

   → Are you doubting your abilities or confidently charging forward?

   → What language are you using?

   → Do your statements include the words "always," "never," "impossible," "can't," "should," "shouldn't," "must," or "mustn't"?

   → What limiting belief statement can you reframe?

2. Limiting beliefs often pop up when we're trying to set a goal. We're aware that something needs to change but, as we start making a plan to take decisive Action, a thought pops into our head that shuts down our goal before we even begin. In Table 1, I provide some examples of limiting beliefs you may encounter when setting goals, along with how they might make you feel and a possible reframe to help.

Table 1. *Limiting Beliefs with Reframes*

Goal/Intention	Limiting Belief	Resulting Feeling	Possible Reframe
I will get this done today.	*You'll never get this all done.*	Overwhelmed	*I'll get as much done as I can. I'll start with one thing.*
I will exercise four times this week.	*It's already Wednesday, you'll never do it. You might as well start next week.*	All or nothing; defeated	*I'll exercise today and then put exercise into my schedule at least two more times.*
I will get Fred to help me.	*People always let me down.*	Isolated, unsupported	*I'll ask Fred if he can help me or if he knows someone else who can.*

Our beliefs, values, and habits feed our thoughts, which then feed our feelings and our actions.

Notice your thoughts. Determine whether they're really true or are just limiting beliefs and/or stories you've made up. Whatever you believe is important. Whatever changes you want to make, it's time to believe that you can. Don't believe everything you think.

Questions to ask yourself:

- → What thoughts am I having that might be limiting, negative, or problem-focused?
- → How are my feelings (anxiety, fear, overwhelm) fed by the thoughts I perpetuate?
- → What results do I really want? What is one thought that limits my ability to achieve them?

DIAL UP, DIAL DOWN

Situations and actions can influence our thoughts too. Let's look at all the moments that make up our day as though they're turning a dial on a **Judge-O-Meter**. If we start in the neutral position and then accomplish something we determine is good, we generally feel better about ourselves. The dial goes up. Think of it like putting gas in our tanks. If we do something that isn't received well or perceive something we do as "not good enough" or "bad," we generally feel worse about ourselves. The dial goes down and our tanks become emptier.

Every Action we take has a consequence in our lives. We interpret things, judge ourselves and others, and try to make sense of all we experience. However, most moments in our day don't move the dial in either direction, especially if we aren't used to celebrating small wins. Many people look at their to-do lists at the end of the day and give themselves a hard time about what didn't get done. What if, at the end of the day, you celebrated all the steps you *did* take?

Exercise 19: Dial Up, Dial Down

Imagine where your Judge-O-Meter dial might be. Make your own list of things that make your dial go up and down. Table 2 provides some examples to get you started.

Table 2. *Examples of Dialing Up and Dialing Down*

Dial Up	Dial Down
I check something off my to-do list.	I avoid doing that thing I hate to do.
I have a great conversation with someone.	I have a conflict-filled talk with a loved one.
I get ready for something way ahead of time.	I'm late for a meeting.
Someone thanks me for something I did.	No one noticed how hard I worked on something.
I try something and succeed.	I try something difficult and fail.*
I celebrate all that I accomplished, even if I didn't succeed this time.	I put myself down for not accomplishing the full list.

* For most, failure is the end of the line. They pack up their toys and head home. Let's reframe the word *fail* into the acronym FAIL: first attempt in learning. It means that we gained some information but there's still room to grow. I invite you to turn your failures into learning experiences. What could you do better or differently next time?

Fear

Our minds and our hearts are not always aligned. If fear finds its way into our emotions and thoughts, any heart's desire or strong Mindset can quickly disappear. It's better to be prepared.

FEAR = False Evidence Appearing Real

Fear is a sign that something matters to us. Just as with our thoughts, we need to accept that our fears might not be rooted in reality. Even the feeling of being overwhelmed is rooted in fear. It may be fear you can't handle it all or fear that you'll start with the wrong thing and let something else drop. Fear is at the root of almost all hesitation. Some level of fear will likely show up when you decide on a goal, so take the time now to decide what you'll do about it. Fear is the obstacle you want to make peace with as you take your journey. Notice I didn't say "before" you take your journey. If we wait until things are perfect—ready and set—we'll never get going!

What would you think and how would you feel if you were suddenly asked to speak to a group of thirty strangers? Would your first reaction be fear or excitement? Something out of a comfort zone might be interpreted as exciting to one person and horrifying to someone else. Some people love speaking in front of others and want to get better at it, while others do anything in their power not to—even to a small group.

Which came first, the emotion (fear), the feeling (desperation), or the thought (*I don't want to do this*)? I'm going to refer to a definition from Think Psych to help untangle all this: First we're exposed to an event (stimulus), then our brains immediately sense it as either a threat or a reward, then we have an emotional response such as fear, sadness, anger, or excitement. "Emotions are the biological and chemical reactions in our bodies in response to an internal or external trigger" (Leonhardt 2022). Part of the brain's response may cause physical changes as well, such as an increased heart rate or sweaty palms. After a slight delay, the mind interprets the situation and we have a feeling—a mental interpretation of the emotion and the circumstances. In one person, a visceral emotion of fear may lead to an interpretation of desperation, while in another, the fear of being asked to speak may morph into a feeling of excitement and then curiosity. It all depends on the way they talk themselves through it.

For purposes of your success and happiness, the most important thing to remember is to be aware of your thoughts, emotions, and feelings. Question your thoughts, and don't assume what you're thinking is a true reflection of reality. If you add a pause between the stimulus and your response, you'll be able to have more control over what happens next. Will you take actions that support your goals and get the results you want, or will you stay reactive and on autopilot?

Have you ever considered taking on a big project outside of your comfort zone? Think of two examples, one you achieved and one you didn't. What thoughts inspired you to achieve it?

- ❖ *I know why this is important to me.*
- ❖ *I want to make a change.*
- ❖ *I'll take this one step at a time and, little by little, I'll get there.*
- ❖ *I'll recruit an accountability buddy.*
- ❖ *I can do this!*
- ❖ *It doesn't have to be perfect.*
- ❖ *I can find the answers, or I can find help.*

Now let's look at a challenging goal that you didn't achieve. What kept you from achieving your goal? Did fear play a part? Once you identify that fear, you'll probably identify the Mindset that has driven your Action or inaction. What was your fear?

- Failure
- Rejection
- The unknown
- Succeeding, and all the changes that might happen if I did
- Talking honestly with someone; being vulnerable
- Being ridiculed or ignored
- Feeling not good enough or capable enough
- Proving all my worst fears true
- Giving something up
- Getting out of my comfort zone

Exercise 20: Face Your Fears

What is your current goal?

1. Name the thoughts that will make this goal more successful.
2. Name the fears that are embedded in this goal and the thoughts you have about them.

Focus on the first list, not the second!

When fear is present, ask yourself, *What am I afraid of?* Keep asking again and again until you find your true answer. You'll discover the rationalizations, the excuses, and the lighter versions of the truth until you see what's at the core. Read my examples from my own life with the questions I've asked myself, then write your own:

- *Am I afraid of launching projects because they might fail, or is it really that I'm afraid they'll be so successful I might get too busy?*
- *Am I afraid of never finishing my book, or is it really that I'm afraid it won't be good enough and no one will buy it?*
- *Am I afraid that I don't have the right words to say, or is it really that I'm afraid of what could happen no matter what I say? What if it causes more conflict?*

Am I afraid of (_____), or is it really (_____)?

THOUGHTS. FEELINGS. ACTIONS. RESULTS.

Something happens in your life, and it starts a chain reaction of thoughts. For the sake of this discussion, let's look at four variables in this order:

Thoughts → Feelings → Actions → Results

Using these four words, you can crack the code of guiding your thoughts to work for you instead of against you. Ask yourself, "How are my thoughts affecting my feelings, actions, and results?" It's a well-known methodology used in cognitive behavioral therapy, a type of talk therapy. As the Mayo Clinic (n.d.) states, "CBT helps you become aware of inaccurate or negative thinking so you can view challenging situations more clearly and respond to them in a more effective way." This concept has become so mainstream that it's the focal point of hundreds of self-help books, articles, and programs, including Linda Larsen's work on self-esteem, which we'll learn more about in the next section.

> **You can't always choose your thoughts, but you can decide whether to listen to them.**

Our thoughts about any given issue, challenge, or obstacle affect our feelings, which in turn affect our behaviors or actions, which ultimately affect our results. When you feel engulfed in negative emotions, when you're taking ineffective Action, or when you aren't getting the results you want, go backward in the formula to see what has happened. Looking at your thoughts can help you reveal the true issue. Because your thoughts are the interpretation of a situation and aren't necessarily based on reality, you'd probably find many limiting and negative thoughts if you were to transcribe your thoughts for a day or two. Most likely they've led to negative feelings, and your actions have become more reactive and less proactive.

You could be thinking, *I don't know where to start*, *This is too hard*, or *He should have...* Those thoughts lead to poor results. I've created Table 3 to illustrate the four variables in a chain reaction of thoughts using a typical challenge we all face: completing a project.

Table 3. *The Thoughts to Results Cycle*

What Are You Thinking?	How Does That Make You Feel?	What Actions Do You Take?	**What Results Do You Get?**
I want to get this project done, but I don't know where to start!	Overwhelmed and anxious.	Very few steps taken, mostly avoiding the project.	None. This leads me to feel behind and ashamed or embarrassed.

If you fill in this type of chart while you're feeling stuck, start by writing down your thoughts, then explore how those thoughts made you feel, what steps you took, and what your current results are. If you're feeling overwhelmed and are avoiding a project, then your results will be lackluster. You can see that each variable builds upon the next. Reviewing your situation this way is a post-Action Reflection of what you experienced.

But what if there was a more proactive way to achieve your desired outcomes? You can use this same formula to get your desired results by flipping the chart and putting your desired results in the first column. Then, brainstorm the actions you'd need to take to achieve your desired outcome, the feelings that would help you act, and the thoughts that would support those feelings. As you're brainstorming, you don't have to write out your ideas in a linear fashion. You may think of a first step to take, put that in the Action column, and then decide what thoughts could motivate you to take that Action. You can also start with the thoughts column and pepper it with positive thoughts about the project or issue.

I filled out a chart like this with a group in which one member wanted to pursue a big project. We kept a running list of actions, feelings, and thoughts that would boost her success—in no particular order. The one column that was consistent for almost any desired outcome was the positivity they wanted to feel to complete the goal (belief, commitment, confidence, clarity, focus, excitement, and motivation, to name a few).

Let me share an example that many entrepreneurs can relate to: launching a new website. It may feel extremely daunting, but if you brainstorm the answers you know and can speculate what thoughts and feelings might help you accomplish your goal, you'll begin to see results something like those in Table 4.

Table 4. *The Results Cycle (RAFT)*

Result (Desired Outcome)	Actions to Achieve	Positive Feelings	Thoughts to Boost Me
Launch a new website	❖ Look at other websites in my niche ❖ Research and select a platform (WordPress, Wix, etc.) ❖ Determine and buy the domain name ❖ Outline the website with pages I want ❖ Write the copy ❖ Decide whether to hire an editor or web designer ❖ Select photos/graphics ❖ Get feedback from people I trust	❖ Committed ❖ Belief in myself and the project ❖ Confident ❖ Excited ❖ Thrilled ❖ Dedicated ❖ Focused ❖ Thorough ❖ Motivated ❖ Inspired ❖ Clear about what I want and need	❖ *Remember my why* ❖ *I don't have to do it alone* ❖ *This is a great idea* ❖ *This will help me grow my business* ❖ *I can ask for help* ❖ *I've done some of this before; I can do it again* ❖ *One step at a time!*

Exercise 21: Build Your RAFT

Now it's your turn. Using Table 5, fill in your desired outcome for one or two goals, then ask yourself what possible steps you need to take to achieve them, the positive feelings you want to feel, and the thoughts to support you in reaching your desired outcome. You don't have to fill in one column before you go to the next. Just start anywhere to get your mind flowing. When you're done, you'll have a **RAFT**, a roadmap of your results, actions, feelings, and thoughts, to guide you to Completion. If you brainstorm two similar goals at the same time, you may notice the similarity between your answers in the feelings and thoughts columns. *I can do this* is always a helpful thought!

Table 5. *Blank Results Cycle (RAFT)*

Result (Desired Outcome)	Actions to Achieve	Positive Feelings	Thoughts to Boost Me
Goal #1			
Goal #2			

If you're used to putting yourself last, you might self-sabotage: *It's not important; I'll make up for it later.* Catch yourself in those moments. Shift your thinking to develop new neural pathways and healthier thought patterns. Allow your Best Self to take charge and stand up for you. Also, catch yourself in the moments when you're getting the results you want, behaving effectively, and feeling positive. What types of thoughts come to you before all of that happens? Perhaps they're curious, confident, and compassionate like these:

- ❖ *I wonder what might happen if I try this out.*
- ❖ *If I keep working on this one step at a time, my life will be better.*
- ❖ *I've learned a lot going through this; taking care of myself is my first priority.*

Your thoughts are your power, the key to your success.

Steven J. Fogel (2014) refers to this way of thinking as an attitude he calls **COAL**, which stands for being curious, open, accepting, and loving toward ourselves. This helps us practice a mindful thought process that supports our growth. Using **affirmations**, a type of positive thought, also gives us the fuel we need to move our feelings and actions toward our desired outcomes.

There are many affirmations you can turn to as a resource for empowering thoughts. State them in the present tense like this:

- ❖ *I am thorough, organized, and strategic.*
- ❖ *I can make anything happen.*
- ❖ *I take loving care of myself.*

Wait, did any of those affirmations trip you up? Did the Judge's voice flare up inside of you? *Who are you kidding? You're not thorough, organized, or strategic! You couldn't make a dog bark right now, and you have no time for self-care!* Thankfully, I've found a tool for resolving these affirmation dilemmas. It comes (with her permission) from Linda Larsen's audio CD set, *12 Secrets to High Self-Esteem* (2001). Try adding the small phrase "At my finest and best, I am" to the beginning of your list of affirmations, qualities, and characteristics. You might say something like, "At my finest and best, I am organized," at which point your Judge may want to immediately contradict your assertion. If this happens, remind yourself of just one time you were organized, tidy, or prepared ahead of time. Then you could say, "I've done it in the past, and I can do it again."

At your finest and best, you may be a lot of things that you may not feel you are on your worst day. Using Larsen's phrase over and over again allows your mind to hear the truth and believe what you're saying. Think back to a situation when you were at your finest and best. Relive that moment. Feel the strength you had in the past that's still inside of you now. You can summon that version of yourself and be that way again by using an affirmation that embodies who you were at that moment: *At my finest and best, I am strategic, loving, funny, curious, creative, and more.*

When I let my Best Self take control, I am my finest and best. I know that I can tackle my office, complete a big project one step at a time, and handle a stressful situation as it happens. I believe I can create time for self-care to support a calmer, happier version of myself. As I say those things, my mind looks for ways to make them real, giving me examples of ways I can make the statements true. I can do X to tackle my office. I can do Y to treat myself to some downtime. I can do or say Z when I'm feeling a little stressed.

Exercise 22: Create Your Finest and Best List

Create a finest and best list for yourself.

At my finest and best I (am/can) _____.

Write at least ten statements, and be creative!

Noticing Your Mindset

Have you ever made a situation bigger in your mind than it was in reality? Did you avoid it and never accomplish whatever you set out to do? It might've been only a small step, but in your mind you imagined it to be a giant leap. Sometimes our minds can play tricks on us. The parts that hold us back fill our minds with potential obstacles that make things seem more difficult or even impossible. We need to remember that what seems like a mountain could in reality be just a molehill. It all depends on our Mindset—the way we're looking at the situation.

A few years back, I was feeling busy but like I wasn't making much progress toward my goals. I had my coaching practice and family events, then suddenly had to become a Zoom expert when COVID-19 began. (It was a whirlwind, and I'm sure many of you also had your own chaos around that time.) I felt trapped in a chaotic life, but I had so much more to accomplish.

During a coaching session—yes, coaches have coaches—I spoke to my coach about wanting clarity. I needed to figure out the next steps for my coaching business and my professional interests. I wanted to pay attention to several incomplete projects, including finishing writing my book, launching more classes, and expanding my coach mentoring niche. My Mindset was, *I will eventually do them all, but who knows when.*

The first win of the session was identifying just one thing to focus on. This gave me a clear target for my energy, and I chose to relaunch my newsletter. The second win was my determination to hire my friend and marketing consultant, Jocelyn Murray, to help me get this done. My Awareness showed me from past endeavors that I do my best with an accountability partner. There were also some technical issues involving my website that were holding me back, and I knew she could help me with them.

I shifted my Mindset to, *I will get this done, one project at a time, one step at a time, with partners to encourage and guide me when I need help.* When I spoke with Jocelyn, I told her I was ready to take a big leap. Her response was, "It's not a big leap; it's just a step over a little puddle." Jocelyn had powerfully reframed my thinking! That's when I knew I had been making a mountain out of a molehill, a giant ocean out of a little puddle. This was one small step in a series of steps, and I could complete them one at a time. I went from using language that was draining my energy and closing off possibilities to using language that encompassed ease and flow while being decisive with my actions. This process was something I'd done with many, many clients, and now I had someone to help me do it for myself.

Ultimately, I got my newsletter going, and I've published an average of twelve per year ever since. With Jocelyn's help, I shifted from doubtful to decisive and took Action all the way to the Completion of the first newsletter. Since this was an ongoing goal, I had to spend time reflecting on how to maintain it moving forward. I got past that initial block in order to get the first one going, then I just had to repeat the process over and over until it felt like second nature.

This is what I learned after taking time for Reflection, the eighth and last step of the Action Cycle:

- ❖ I get overwhelmed when I think about all the projects I want to get done.
- ❖ When I have many things I want to accomplish, I am more successful if I prioritize them and then start with one at a time.
- ❖ A helpful Mindset is: *One project at a time, one step at a time.*

General helpful tips:

- ❖ Take any big project and break it down into smaller steps. Once you decide on the first step, it makes achieving the next step and the step after that much more likely.
- ❖ Action, any Action, is better than standing still. If the first step isn't the right one, that's okay. Remember that you can shift your path at any time.
- ❖ It's okay to ask for help. Having an accountability partner, a coach, or someone to talk to as you find your new perspective might be exactly the kind of support you need.
- ❖ Be mindful of the way you speak to yourself. Use positive, compassionate, and committed language to get the best results. Your thoughts matter.

CHAPTER 6
INNER SELF

> IFS [Internal Family Systems] recognizes that underneath all our parts, every human being has a true Self that is wise, deep, strong, and loving. This is who we truly are when we aren't being hijacked by the painful or defensive voices of our parts.
>
> —Jay Early and Bonnie Weiss, *Freedom from Your Inner Critic: A Self-Therapy Approach*

- Explore Your Inner Parts
- A Comparison of Parts Work
- Procrastination
- Flow

I believe our inner self is a system comprised of the Self—who we are at our core—as well as aspects of ourselves that have thoughts and emotions that drive our actions. Some of these aspects, or "parts," as they'll be called throughout the book, are really helpful and motivating, but other parts may derail us. We can have conflicting parts that keep us stuck and ramp up our anxiety. Is your Perfectionist battling with your Achiever? Does your Pleaser take over when a part of you wants to set up boundaries?

The more we ignore the paradox within ourselves, the more conflicted we feel. One of the greatest benefits of understanding our inner Self is being able to identify our conflicting inner parts. Then we can do the work to bring them into our Awareness so that we can be more at choice, intentionally choosing how to respond to a situation. This is a fairly complicated process and is usually facilitated by a trained therapist or coach, though, as we can see from this chapter's epigraph, Internal Family Systems believes most people are capable of teaching themselves this process. For the purpose of this book, I want to identify some concepts about parts work and offer tools you can use to shift yourself from doubtful to decisive—from stuck to taking Action.

EXPLORE YOUR INNER PARTS

As we did in the previous chapter, we can look at our actions and get a sense of what thoughts are driving us. If the Action is perfectionism, what are the thoughts and feelings that drive that Action? Now let's add inner parts. Can you name the part of your inner Self that thinks that way? Perhaps we'll just call it the Perfectionist. There can be judgmental parts that inhibit us from reaching our goals, compulsive parts that push us toward perfection, and expansive parts that encourage us to live our Best Life. Our results are influenced by the net sum of our parts—timid and bold, weak and strong, angry and happy—as well as our Best Self. Which parts do you want to dial into and understand better so that you can end the back-and-forth conflict and move toward a happier life?

We have access to our Best Self when all the parts with their derailing thoughts are quiet. Our Best Self is expansive and joyful rather than reactive and anxious. Our inner parts each have their own desires that at times may not align with what will benefit us the most. All these parts combine to create our inner Self, and with a deeper understanding of them we can find balance, accomplish goals, and live a life of ease and flow.

It's important to understand all the parts that make up our inner Self. We need to be aware and accepting but also be able to turn the volume up or down on each part. Finding this balance allows us to let our Best Self run the show. I've struggled with one part of my inner Self my whole life: my Avoider comes out whenever I have trouble making a decision or feel overwhelmed. When I do things for others, I can work to overcome my Avoider, but when it's all for me I tend to struggle. I give in to the more challenging, doubtful aspects of my inner Self. Although I've been able to dial down my Avoider, I want to share a typical example of when it does show up for me.

As I wrote this book, I found parts of myself in constant battle. The Avoider, Taskmaster, Judge, and Best Self are just a few parts that were at odds with each other. Each chimed in with their own thoughts that caused me to feel and do divergent, occasionally frustrating things. Sometimes I gave up and found myself zoning out with YouTube videos. Other times I found myself diligently cleaning the house instead of writing. The more negative my thoughts were, the less I wrote. It's not hard to guess which part would be most likely to help me achieve my goal (see Table 6).

Table 6. *My Inner Parts Battle*

Inner Part	Thoughts	Feelings	Actions
Avoider	*I don't know what to write. I have other things I have to do.*	Hesitant, frustrated, anxious.	I'll do anything but write!
Taskmaster	*Get to work; you can do this!*	Pushed and annoyed at myself.	I may sit at the computer, but I find other things to do.
Judge	*If your outline was in better shape you could finish this thing!*	Unworthy.	I struggle to perfect my outline and never get into a flow state.
Best Self	*I love this topic and have many great ideas to share. I'll set aside an hour this morning to work on it.*	Inspired, calm.	My writing flows from me. I leave the editing for later.

Exercise 23: Reach Your Inner Parts

Now it's your turn. Try this experiment to learn more about your own inner parts, thoughts, feelings, and actions.

1. Name a big goal, one that would cause you to stretch out of your comfort zone.
2. Notice what thoughts come up that are motivating you to reach this goal. See if you can name the parts within you based on what they're saying. Is this your Best Self?
3. Notice how long it takes to go from excited to fearful or doubtful—perhaps a matter of minutes. Is it still your Best Self, or have inner parts arrived? Who are they? For example, if I'm a business owner and want to reach out to potential clients, I might talk myself out of it because it's scary, unknown, and makes me feel vulnerable with a fear of rejection.

Going through this type of inner turmoil is normal for any human being. That's because inner parts exist within all of us, often trying to protect us even if misguided in doing so. Depending on which part we listen to, we might reach out and build our network, or we might give up before we've even begun. Then we'll probably feel regret or shame as we think, *I never do what I really want to be doing.* We might even stay active for weeks in a row, and then life gets in the way and we stop. Our Judge has a field day when we mess up!

Our fearful anxious parts make mountains out of molehills while they try to protect us. They may be trying to stop us from making mistakes, getting rejected, or disappointing others. Our enthusiastic parts see the big picture and are excited to get going. Sometimes they get too excited or overcommitted. They may encourage us to try to do too much or strive for perfection. It's a little like Goldilocks finding the right-sized bed. Play too small, and your life isn't very satisfying. Play too big, and you could be filled with overwhelm and stress. Finding what feels *just right* takes Awareness and practice.

Society has started to normalize inner parts beyond the old perception of them. A clever commercial features a woman who just bought a new car. She rides in it with three other versions of herself, each one focusing on a special feature. One likes the massage seats, and another likes the fabulous sound system. The cautious part fears the Wi-Fi password isn't safe enough. When we do anything in life, such as buying a car, for example, we bring all our parts with us.

The movie *Inside Out* by Disney's Pixar takes this idea to a whole new level. While it's an animated movie meant for children, many adults also enjoy it. The film normalizes and gives insight into the inner parts we all have, as well as their dialogue. The characters are each named after their main emotion—Joy, Sadness, Fear, Anger, and Disgust—which can be thought of as subpersonalities of the human child's main character, Riley. The five main parts disagree on how to deal with Riley's cross-country move—a big change—and chaos ensues. Joy always speaks in a positive way, supporting Riley, while Sadness, Anger, Fear, and Disgust represent Riley's negative thinking.

Have you gone through a big life change in which Joy was battling it out with Sadness or Fear? What were the circumstances? Was it when you were married, started a new business, or moved across the country? The paradox between Joy and Fear exists in every one of us.

A Comparison of Parts Work

I've studied three coaching programs that include a structure based on inner parts: **Internal Family Systems (IFS)**, **The Power of TED* (*The Empowerment Dynamic)®**, and **Positive Intelligence.** As a guide to explore the parts that might be helping or hindering you, I'd like to share a little bit of what I've personally learned from each of these programs. I'll approach this from what these programs have in common, as well as how I've used them to help explore my own and my clients' inner landscapes of thoughts and feelings. If the topics interest you, I encourage you to read more about these three programs.

All three of these structures or coaching methods could be considered a type of parts work and have some similar concepts at their core. Our inner parts influence our lives in many ways. Our actions are driven by our thoughts and emotions, which are influenced by the balance between our Best Self and the strength of our parts that might motivate or derail us. How motivated we are at any given moment is influenced by that balance. Some of those parts have become ingrained as part of our habits and default ways of thinking, and they're present even when we aren't triggered.

Think of a time when something scary or urgent happened. During the most stressful moments, have you said or done things you regretted later? You were acting on an adrenaline rush stemming from specific areas of your brain designed to keep you alive. Instead of forming calm, rational thoughts, your brain and body were acting on instinct. That's your **Survivor Brain** at work. It can save your life, and it can also cause problems.

All three programs attempt to identify when that primitive, reactive Survivor Brain is in charge and then reframe our thinking. That's harder than it sounds until you've done it often enough. Getting from Survivor Brain to Best Self takes Awareness, presence, and some sort of calming activity that will get you out of your Survivor Brain and back into neutral. Something like deep breathing, taking a walk outdoors, or meditating can facilitate the shift. You have to be aware of the thoughts you're having, turn down the volume of the ineffective thoughts, and turn up the volume of your new perspective or Mindset.

One gift of learning about our inner parts is gaining the ability to have more Awareness and make conscious choices, becoming the drivers of our cars rather than the passengers. This makes us less vulnerable and more resilient as our reactive parts show up less often. When I'm filled with doubt and fear, I know it isn't my Best Self's thoughts. I could name that part Fear, Doubt, or Perfectionist. That's another gift of doing parts work: I can reframe to saying, "A *part* of me is really doubtful" or "A *part* of me feels hesitant, vulnerable, or insecure" rather than "*I* am really doubtful." This allows me to see that it's not my Best Self in control at that moment. I can breathe, calm myself down, and then move forward as my Best Self.

IFS was founded by Richard C. Schwartz, PhD, a family therapist and academic who created the model as a response to clients' descriptions of their own inner parts. He teaches that we all have parts within us, as well as an entity called the "Self," or what I call our Best Self. The IFS model uses the term "**blended**" to indicate that "the feelings and beliefs of one part have merged with another part of the Self" (Schwartz 2023, 151)—that is, their presence is blocking our capacity to be in the essence of our true Self; these parts and their emotions are running the show. The goal is to be "unblended," or separated, so that all parts can be understood and we can let our true Self come forward (Anderson, Sweezy, and Schwartz 2017, 5). We acknowledge the parts' concerns, but we ask those parts to step back to allow our true Self to emerge with its many stable and wonderful qualities, including being calm, curious, courageous, and compassionate.

I think of it this way: Our Best Self is always at our core, like a compass always pointing north. It's available to lead us forward during any challenge and help us take advantage of opportunities as they arise. Unfortunately, our Best Self is often clouded over by our inner parts, so using the tools in this book, particularly the Action Cycle, can help your Best Self shine through. Ideally, it's your Best Self making the choice to start or stop doing something.

Some of your parts have good qualities that you may not always feel, such as bravery or conversational skills. You can call on your brave part to be with you as you tackle a big issue, or you can ask the part of you that's warm and curious to be with you as you network at the next business meeting. Your Best Self is within you not only during your daily life but also when you're most challenged. The trick is knowing when you're acting as your Best Self and when you're not. If you find yourself metaphorically sitting in neutral, stuck in a negatively charged rut, or driving in reverse full of fear or avoidance, then you clearly aren't acting as your Best Self.

One of the most authentic descriptions I've heard that references our parts comes from a podcast with Richard Schwartz and Elizabeth Gilbert, the latter of whom is the author of *Eat Pray Love*. Gilbert said that when she's trying to be creative and her fearful part shows up, she "asks it to get in the back seat of the minivan while we go on the trip together"; her parts can be around her but not in charge (Sounds True 2023). We don't want our doubtful parts or hesitant parts to be at the wheel when we're making decisions. We want our Best Self in control.

Our Parts Influence Our Relationships

As described by Dr. Stephen Karpman in 1964, we can play three roles in relationships, which he calls the "Drama Triangle" (Center for The Empowerment Dynamic, n.d.a.). Those three parts are the Victim, the Persecutor, and the Rescuer. Imagine something bad happens and your perception is, *I'm being persecuted. Another person or the universe is conspiring against me, making my life miserable.* You could believe that thought, but it's important to check its validity.

When you're a Victim, you believe you need someone or something to be your Rescuer to help you solve your problem. This puts your happiness into the hands of someone else rather than your own, disabling you from solving the problem yourself. This extreme way of thinking typically happens on a subtle level, but it exists just the same. We rescue our kids and blame others or society as a whole for persecuting us. Then we act out in Persecutor-like ways when things aren't going well.

I have all this insight on the subject because there was a time when I was living as a Victim. I truly felt certain people were persecuting me, and I kept looking outside myself to be rescued. Then I found the book *The Power of TED* (*The Empowerment Dynamic)*® by David Emerald, and my life shifted a full 180 degrees. The Empowerment Dynamic gives us three roles to replace the Victim, Persecutor, and Rescuer roles of the Karpman triangle: the Creator, the Challenger, and the Coach (Emerald 2015). We sit in each of these roles at any given moment, and we see others around us as holding these roles too: *I am the Creator of my life. I am the Challenger asking others and myself to be their best. I embody the Coach in the way I deal with myself and others.*

We can tell what Drama Triangle role we are in by looking at our focus, intentions, and behavior. The Victim gets anxious and ineffective from focusing on the problem. At its worst, the Victim stews in all the ways that life isn't fair, ever complaining and never seeing a way out. It dials up the drama in life like someone picking at a scab so that it never heals. The Victim feels and acts like a Victim, saying Victim-generated things and feeling Victim-generated feelings, thinking life or others around it are persecuting it. Sometimes the Victim takes on the Persecutor's role and behaves in a way that feels like it's fighting back (seemingly thinking that it's winning), but it's actually making matters worse. Meanwhile, the Victim wished that someone or something would magically rescue it: *Calgon, take me away!*

Here's an example of three different parts as they interpret the same situation. As you read, think about how these thought patterns make you feel and what you might do as a result.

Challenge: I'm trying to lose weight, and my husband has dessert after dinner every night.

1. **Victim**: *It's not fair. I miss my desserts. I'm going to have some too.*
2. **Persecuted Victim**: *How could he do that in front of me when he knows I've given up dessert after dinner?*
3. **Creator**: *What's my opportunity? I can save some of my calories during the day for an after-dinner treat and pick something without too much sugar. I'll build my self-control and not feel deprived. I can also just say no and feel proud of myself.*

Did you notice that the Creator doesn't judge or feel victimized? It creatively gives itself a few options.

In a TED*-inspired world, each of us is the Creator of our lives, able to determine our own destinies. We focus on what we want and what we have control over, and we look at our obstacles as challenges to overcome (not persecution). Sometimes we take on the role of the Challenger to help others around us or the Coach to help them find their own solutions, just as we find our own. We can ask those around us to be our Coach rather than our Rescuer. We can also talk to ourselves in a more Coach- or Creator-like way. On any given day, in any situation, we can adopt these roles to be our Best Self.

In our current society, some parents are described as "helicopter parents," those who hover over their children in an attempt to protect them from the hard realities of life. When parents rescue their children too often and try to prevent them from ever feeling loss, failure, or accountability, they're actually treating their children like Victims who are unable to take care of themselves or learn new skills. These children learn to blame others or feel disempowered rather than ever owning and creating their own happiness. The same can be said about adults who rescue their friends, loved ones, or coworkers.

As Table 7 illustrates, the Mindset of a Victim is much different from the Mindset of a Creator; their thoughts lead to different feelings, actions, and results.

Table 7. *Victim versus Creator*

Role	Thoughts	Feelings	Actions	Results
Victim	This is hard. Why me?	Anxious, Incapable	Inconsistent or no Action; lash out as the Persecutor	Negative
Creator	I will begin here. I can do this.	Confident	Baby steps	Forward Action

Having an Awareness of myself, I know which thoughts work better for me. If I catch myself thinking negatively,

I shift my thinking and reframe. I stop, take a few deep breaths, and get curious about what parts might be stirred up, and I seek out the best Creator Mindset to achieve my desired outcome. Reframing your thinking is like asking a negative part to step back and allow a stronger, more positive part to take over.

Discover Your Saboteurs

Another program that does a great job of revealing our inner parts and encouraging reframing is the Positive Intelligence program, which was created by Shirzad Chamine. The inspiration for Chamine's work, much like David Emerald's, came from personal experience and exploration. For Chamine, there were a few key moments in his life, actual interventions, when others told him he was being harshly judgmental toward those around him (Chamine 2012, 10–11). There's nothing like a rude awakening or potential loss of a relationship to make us look at ourselves in the mirror and see our blind spots: *Ah, that's how you see me? Is that really true?*

With self-reflection, Chamine realized that he saw the world through the lens of his Judge. He began to notice how often he criticized himself, others, and all of life's circumstances. He knew he had to do something about it, and his Positive Intelligence program was the result. He spent many years studying the areas of neuroscience, positive psychology, cognitive behavioral psychology, and performance science. In improving his own self-management and internal dialogue, he created a program that has helped tens of thousands of people, including me. Short of paraphrasing his whole book, which I highly recommend, and with his permission, I will share with you the nuts and bolts of Positive Intelligence.

Our lives are influenced by the negative parts we all experience (Saboteurs). After much research, Chamine identified the Judge and its nine Accomplice Saboteurs that he feels are the root of all negative parts we experience: the Avoider (that's me!), the Controller, the Hyper-Achiever, the Hyper-Rational, the Hyper-Vigilant, the Pleaser, the Restless (another one of my top Saboteurs), the Stickler, and the Victim.

We also have a wise-knowing part he calls the Sage (which I call my Best Self and Emerald calls the Creator). It is the relationship between the two diametrically opposed forces of the Saboteurs and the Sage that affects our ability to reach success and happiness. Our positive intelligence quotient (PQ), a term Chamine created, refers to the percentage of time "our minds are acting as our friend rather than our enemy." Ideally, we want our score to be at least seventy-five out of one hundred.

Our minds are our friends when we function from the Sage-related parts of our brain rather than the Survivor Brain. By incorporating education, mindfulness, and meditative techniques, Chamine's program helps us more frequently function from our Sage brain and increase our PQ scores. The program focuses on three core strategies:

1. Weaken the Saboteurs—gain the ability to notice and interrupt when a Saboteur is present.
2. Strengthen your PQ brain muscles—the parts of the brain that help you thrive.
3. Strengthen the Sage—gain the ability to choose your thoughts and actions from the Sage's perspective: "Every challenge, outcome, and circumstance is a gift or an opportunity" (Chamine 2012, 72).

The biggest takeaway from the program, aside from understanding our Saboteurs and the powers of the Sage, is the ability to use our mental muscles to increase our PQ scores and thereby live happier lives. What he refers to as "mental muscles" are our abilities to be mindful and notice when our thoughts are anxious or negative, to pause and get back in control, and to turn to Sage-like thoughts such as curiosity, exploration, and innovation. Mindfulness at its best! As we get more adept and strengthen our mental muscles, we raise our PQ scores and live with a Sage focus.

I love remembering that I—and all of us—have a Sage at our core. Our Sages can overcome issues and challenges while encouraging us toward success. When we're at our best, life is in a state of flow. We're calm, curious, courageous, and confident, and we're thinking and acting from our Sage brain. We can explore, innovate, and navigate through our lives with more compassion and proactive Action. Over time and with practice, our negative thinking can take up less and less of our executive functioning. When someone says something that might trigger you, notice it, and then make the choice to either act on it or let it go. You're greater than that one comment, situation, or challenge. The Sage in you, your Best Self, can overcome issues and challenges while encouraging you toward success.

Exercise 24: Recognize Your Saboteurs

1. Of the Judge and the nine Saboteurs mentioned in Positive Intelligence, which are most likely to show up when you're stressed or challenged (Avoider, Controller, Victim, Hyper-Achiever, Hyper-Rational, Hyper-Vigilant, Pleaser, Restless, and/or Stickler)?
2. How do they influence your actions?
3. What can you do to help you recognize when your Saboteur has taken over your thoughts and actions?

PROCRASTINATION

You can't talk about being stuck without discussing procrastination. The world is filled with people who are judging themselves for being procrastinators. In my opinion, procrastination is a side effect of the internal battle we have about a given issue. It's a symptom that, if explored properly, can reveal the deep reasons for feeling stuck or hesitant. Once that's resolved, you're less likely to procrastinate and can more readily access decisiveness and Action.

The *Cambridge Dictionary* defines procrastination as "to keep delaying something that must be done, often because it is unpleasant or boring." If one part of me is thinking that I should take care of some unpleasant task, but another part of me isn't sure what step to take, how to do it, or is afraid of the repercussions, then I'm less likely to do it—I'll procrastinate. Just labeling the task "unpleasant" reveals that my Judge has already gotten involved. I'll give myself excuses such as "I'm not ready" or "I have other, more important things to do." When I stop and ask myself why I'm procrastinating, digging deep enough to find an honest answer, I have the opportunity to overcome my hesitation.

No universal answer to overcoming procrastination exists because the cause is different from person to person and situation to situation. What's unpleasant for you might not be unpleasant for others. Conflict, technology, sales, tidiness, household chores, holiday gatherings, business meetings, changing a diet, making decisions, and learning how to market your goods or services are all examples of things that can be unpleasant and lead to procrastination. However, it depends on the person and the circumstances.

In 2010, I was making my daughter an afghan as a wedding gift, which I had previously done for my other two children. I really enjoy the creativity and design aspects of crocheting, and I included my daughter in Assessing options and picking out a pattern. I started the project right away (no procrastination yet), but after a few weeks, I realized the partially finished afghan was just sitting there in front of me while I watched TV at night. Weeks went by and I couldn't figure out why I was avoiding the project. You can imagine all the rationalizing I was doing: *I'll never have time to start a whole new afghan! It'll be fine, just push through the hesitation!* And last but not least, *Just stop being lazy and do it!*

Deciding to take a few moments to unravel the issue (no pun intended), I faced the realization that I wasn't thrilled with the pattern or the yarn. I didn't think it would look good, so I was avoiding it. Once I came to the conscious revelation that I wasn't happy with this version (Awareness), I made the decision to make a new one. I talked with my daughter, and we agreed on a new pattern and yarn. I worked on it almost daily after that and finished the afghan a few months later, just in time for the wedding shower.

Sometimes procrastination is hesitation and there's a reason for it. Other times procrastination is a result of avoidance or being stuck from too much stress or too many options. Taking the time to ask yourself some key questions will at least bring new answers to your consciousness.

Awareness is always the first step toward change.

Many people procrastinate when it comes to handling relationship issues. If you're inclined to prioritize keeping people happy, then you're not going to want to have a difficult conversation with a loved one, set a boundary with an annoying colleague, or share an unpopular opinion at a neighborhood meeting. That doesn't mean that those things don't bother you or aren't important to you. It means that you haven't figured out how to address them in a way that's comfortable. If pushed too far, you might react with an overly emotional response and be in an even more untenable situation.

So when is the right time to act? When the circumstances are challenging, but before you lose your temper, job, friend, or opportunity. Shift your focus by asking yourself why you're feeling this way and what inner part(s) might be sabotaging you. Accept that it's up to you to do something and commit to taking Action. What are you willing to do about it? You can seek a change in the particular issue, or you can do something about your default response to certain situations.

FLOW

Life isn't always painful or full of sabotaging thoughts (thank goodness!). Sometimes we have instances of feeling like all is right with the world. Our lives are on an even keel, and we're in a state of flow, feeling empowered and getting things done. Those glimmering times of flow can be moments, hours, days, or even weeks long.

Being in a state of flow and feeling like we're our Best Self go hand-in-hand. In both cases, we're free from sabotaging and distracting thoughts. In times of flow, we function as our Best Self, using the more executive regions of our brains as well as using our instincts. We're breaking free from the influence of our other parts and replacing them with clarity, decisiveness, commitment, and Action. We're firing on all cylinders and getting things done, and we're setting boundaries with others, holding ourselves accountable, and feeling proud of who we are. We're feeling empowered, accomplished, and, dare I say, successful. Rather than blaming others for our circumstances or focusing on the worst-case scenarios, we're taking initiative and taking charge of our own outcomes, one step at a time.

I want to be my Best Self as often as possible. Over time and with deep Awareness, I've learned to lift the cloud of my inner parts chatter with some success, and I'm tapping into my Best Self more often. On a good day, listen to your thoughts. You might be thinking, *I've got this. I'm on the right track. I'm going to do this one step at a time.* When we're in flow we're also resilient. We're able to overcome challenges without too much drama or too many setbacks, and we can do so with a sense of overall gratitude. We're not only thriving but stepping out of our comfort zones and trying new things.

Did you notice what's missing in times of flow? It's the thoughts and feelings of self-doubt, overwhelm, chaos, fear, and confusion—when our sabotaging parts are in charge of our thinking. When the negative channel takes hold, flow disappears. When the flow is gone, it's a sign that some of our inner parts are derailing us; our Best Self has been nudged away from the steering wheel.

Why is it possible to be in flow in one area of our lives and struggle in another? It depends on which parts are empowered and dominating that area of our lives. Do confidence and expertise live there, or have negative experiences caused a panel of reactive, protective, and negative parts to start running the show? When we feel fear, it's our fearful part that's controlling our thoughts. When we feel doubt, it's our doubtful part that has the microphone: *What if I mess up? This could turn out badly!* We can't just whisk those parts away. Instead, we need to acknowledge that they exist for a reason: to protect us from harm, embarrassment, or some other unfavorable outcome.

The interesting thing is that our parts don't know us as well as we know ourselves. To paraphrase an IFS teaching, our inner parts were formed in our younger years, or after some traumatic experience, as a way to help and protect us. They still imagine us as inexperienced or vulnerable younger selves. They may have the language of a younger version of us, a stern parent, or a past bully. But we've grown beyond those parts, and now it's time to take back the power of our thinking. Our Best Self is in there just begging to come out more often—to be in the flow!

Stuck in a Small Room

I first heard a version of the following story from my priest during a sermon. His moral to the story had a religious theme. Mine will be more metaphysical.

> Sarah and James wanted to get away on vacation. They researched tropical resorts online and found one with photos of large guest rooms, complete with balconies and breathtaking views. Their travel experience getting to the resort, however, was less than relaxing, involving complications and delays.
>
> By the time they arrived at their room, it was late in the evening and they were exhausted. Opening up the hotel door, they were shocked to see a small room with a pull-out couch, a mini fridge, a small window, and an adjoining bathroom. This was nothing like the room they were expecting. Too tired to complain, they made do with the pull-out couch and went to sleep, determined to clear things up in the morning.
>
> After a fitful sleep, Sarah and James went down to the front desk to complain to the clerk. "We

were expecting a gorgeous room with a view and all we got was a pull-out couch!" they exclaimed.

The employee at the front desk asked, "Didn't you open the door to the main room?"

"What main room? We only found a closet."

Sarah and James went back upstairs to see for themselves. Sure enough, in the light of day and with a hint from the hotel clerk, they found the other door and opened it up. With relief and dismay, they saw the main bedroom with a king-sized bed and a balcony with breathtaking views of the beach.

Being stuck in a little room, perhaps with no doors or windows, represents the times when we're triggered, overwhelmed, and unable to logically "find the door" to our big room. The big room represents the place of clear thinking, possibilities, and solutions. It's where you are when you're being your Best Self—calm, outcome-focused, and curious. You're open to ideas and considering all options.

Remember this story when you're feeling doubtful, stuck, or overwhelmed. With emotions like that, you're functioning from your triggered brain. Breathe slowly and deeply for a few minutes, then look for the "door" to your Best Self.

Exercise 25: Identify Your Parts

1. Listen closely to your thoughts, and you'll be able to figure out which parts are in charge at the moment by checking in with your emotions and feelings. Using this chart, fill in the rest of the blanks with a few of your own experiences:

My Positive Parts and Best Self Help Me Feel . . .	My Derailing Inner Parts Cause Me to Feel . . .
Motivated	Discouraged
Supported	Alone
Inspired to take Action	Anxious and overwhelmed
Decisive	Stuck, inactive, hesitant
Excited	Fearful

2. Explore the following:

   → What parts show up when you're challenged?
   → What do those parts tell you, and how do they make you feel?
   → What are your most helpful inner parts?
   → What qualities show up with your helpful parts? Do you experience flow, and are you at your finest and best?
   → How often do you live as a Creator, Challenger, or Coach rather than a Victim, Persecutor, or Rescuer?

Now that you've identified the power of your thoughts, which will you listen to? Challenge and reframe the derailing thoughts into something more empowering. How do they compare with those you experienced during the Dial Up, Dial Down / Judge-O-Meter exercise? Follow the trail of your energy and make intentional choices.

CHAPTER 7
OUR INNER CAST OF CHARACTERS

> By my mid-thirties, I had discovered the powerful Judge and Hyper-Rational Saboteurs, my old invisible survival buddies, and recognized them as my biggest obstacles to greater success and happiness.
>
> —Shirzad Chamine

- Introducing My Cast of Characters
- Positive Inner Parts

How is your current life influenced by your inner cast of characters? You've heard about my key players—Avoider, Restless, and Judge. Now I want you to beckon your curious and knowing parts, as well as your Best Self, to join you for this chapter. The goal is to identify your most active sabotaging parts and begin to paint them as characters in a play. Once you identify when they show up, how they act, and what they typically say, you can begin to defuse their power. You'll more easily reveal their lies and convince them to step back and find other things to do! If you need help, use the Reaching Your Inner Parts exercise from Chapter 6 to revisit who they might be and what they're telling you.

Let's begin by fleshing out your Judge—the master Saboteur. What's it like and when does it show up? Is it typically focused on you or others? Our thoughts reflect the current strength of our Judge and other inner parts. The Judge, also known as the "Inner Critic," criticizes ourselves, others, and situations. If your Judge is very active and empowered, it can be very loud, mean, and hurtful. Chamine called his Judge "the Executioner." You may hear any or all these types of thoughts: *You can't do this! He's a jerk! You're not worthy!* Sometimes, instead of loudly shouting discouraging messages, the Judge's voice can be very subtle, more of a whisper: *That's going to be hard. You probably won't be able to do it.*

Next, let's explore your Judge's accomplices. You know your Saboteurs are running the show when you feel fearful, anxious, shameful, or overwhelmed. The Saboteurs are often trying to eliminate the pain of the problem, not necessarily finding a sustainable solution. Here are a few parts I've seen in myself and my clients over the years:

- ❖ **The Procrastinator, a.k.a. the Avoider.** After the Judge deems something hard, boring, or overwhelming, the Procrastinator finds reasons to delay and "helps" you by finding other things to do instead of the task at hand: *You can start that tomorrow.*
- ❖ **The Perfectionist.** Life is black and white, and this part wants all the ducks to stay in the same row: *No getting out of line! If you're going to do it, you must do it right.* The Perfectionist often prevents you from implementing something because it feels the plan isn't perfect enough or it's not the right time. It might also micromanage because it wants things done in a very specific way.
- ❖ **The Stickler.** When you want to take a bite of a bigger project, this part chimes in to try to convince you to wait until you have time to do it all. It has a very particular way of doing things and lives with many rules about processes and procedures. It may judge others who aren't as detail-oriented. *This is the only way* or *All or nothing* might be its motto.
- ❖ **The Mega-Empathizer.** An overly empathic person tends to worry about everyone and everything else in their life, saving no time, space, or energy for themselves: *I'm okay, but what can I do for you?* Don't get me wrong, I value empathy as much as the next person. The trick here is to dial this part down when it becomes out of balance or when you're worrying about things outside of your control. Focusing more on yourself and what you have control over will put things more in balance and create inner harmony—instead of an ulcer.

- **The Doubter.** Ah, those doubts just slip in at the most inopportune times: *I'm not so sure about that.* Doubters often lack confidence and typically second-guess themselves, especially if they're trying something new or stretching out of their comfort zone. The Doubter thinks about what could go wrong or that another option might be the better one, and it's often in analysis paralysis.

There are many parts within you. Explore your thoughts and identify the ones that are the loudest. It might take a little time to discover the more hidden parts that only come out in very specific situations, but stick with it. There's so much value and insight when you know your inner parts better.

Exercise 26: Outsmart Your Hindering Parts

Name a part of you that's causing trouble for you. Make a pledge to release it so that you can allow your Best Self to be in charge, then fill in the blanks of the following two statements (I've given you some examples):

1. I will no longer be a/an __[People Pleaser, Avoider, Indulger, Perfectionist]__. (In other words, what nagging inner part(s) do you want to dial down?)
2. Instead of being a/an _____, I can _____ and _____.

> ❖ *Instead of being a People Pleaser, I can tell people what I think in a kind manner and still have friends.*
>
> ❖ *Instead of being an Avoider or Indulger, I can do my task and still have time to enjoy myself later. Or better yet, I can make this task more enjoyable.*
>
> ❖ *Instead of being a Perfectionist, I can do my best and it doesn't have to be perfect.*

Perhaps without realizing it, you just created a sentence that you can use as a Mindset. You may need to rewrite your sentence a little differently if the part is still fighting with you. For example, my husband pointed out that some situations require us to be exacting (not a Perfectionist), so your statement might be, "Instead of being a Perfectionist about everything, I'll be exacting when truly necessary and do my best within a reasonable amount of time on everything else."

There are many other potentially chronic problems with a Saboteur at their core. Do you tend to waver when it comes to making decisions? What do you think is behind that? Are there times when you decide to do something but then don't act, start, or finish? What's missing? Do you notice tendencies such as procrastination, perfectionism, micromanagement, or avoidance of conflict when this happens? Who or what are these tendencies serving? These are all challenges stemming from your thinking.

If setting a goal or getting into Action still feels challenging, perhaps your first goal is to focus on the exercises in Chapters 5 and 6 so that you can be more aware of the causes of your struggle. This will allow you to dial down the inhibiting inner parts and strengthen your Best Self. This sounds like a top-level goal to me!

Introducing My Cast

For the last several years, I've been taming a few very strong inner parts besides my Judge. They are my Avoider, Restless, and Indulger. My Avoider and Restless parts keep me chasing after various ideas and avoiding the goals and tasks in my life that get hard or uncomfortable. My Indulger thinks I deserve to take a break and eat some chocolate in every stressful or exciting moment. My life doesn't flow when all those thoughts are taking up space in my mind.

When I get grounded and call on my Best Self, she helps me address the issue, overcome my Avoider and Restless parts, and even quiet my Indulger to a whisper. I like to think of my Best Self as a woman who's figured things out, doesn't sweat the small stuff, is discerning and confident, and knows what she wants. She doesn't always instinctively know how to get to her final destination, but she focuses on all the possibilities until the right answers come.

> One day, I was diligently working at my computer, answering emails, and taking care of tasks on my to-do list. I was working on an email when I started to notice myself standing up. I didn't consciously think, *It's time for a break*, but clearly, my body had that intention.
>
> Here's my interpretation after the fact: My Judge decided this email was too hard to write and it was the wrong time to work on it. My Avoider thought, *Yes, there are other things you could be doing, like taking a walk to the refrigerator*. Restless took charge and signaled the muscles in my legs to stand up and walk away from the computer. Luckily, I intercepted this mindless Action and sat back down at my computer. I told myself, *Finish what you started*.

Your sabotaging parts might show up mindlessly too. Perhaps your Controller or Perfectionist insists you go over the details one more time. Maybe your Pleaser gets triggered when a family member asks for a favor. At times your Indulger or Victim may head to the fridge when you've had a hard day. It's important to get to know what parts are sabotaging your actions with their distorted thoughts.

Exercise 27: Characterize Your Parts

1. Name a goal.
2. Make a list of your inner parts that support your goal and a list of the ones that hinder it.
3. Give those parts some personality with character traits and a motto. Have fun creating the full picture and how they interact.

    a. What is their (possibly distorted) goal?
    b. What are their thoughts about each other and your goal?

4. What is their actual impact on your desired outcome? For example, if your goal was to eat healthier, your list might include helpful parts such as Meal Planner, Veggie Lover, and Healthy Hannah, and hindering parts such as Indulger, Sweets-a-Holic, and Junk Food Jennie.

Positive Inner Parts

If we're facing our negative parts, it's only fair to acknowledge our positive parts as well. When we're in front of a room full of people and have to give a presentation, make a toast, or announce something important, isn't it great when our Courageous, Humorous, and/or Leader parts show up?

According to the IFS model, there are eight characteristics of the Self, or the Eight Cs: calm, clarity, confidence, connection, courage, compassion, creativity, and curiosity (Internal Family Systems Institute, n.d.a.). If you embody and explore any one of these characteristics within yourself, you can find a new approach to a problem or focus on the next best step to take. You may or may not have any of these characteristics at any given moment, but the more often you consciously practice them, the more often you'll feel like your Best Self.

Other examples of positive parts are the four personality types from the PeopleMap system (Leader, People, Task, and Free Spirit). I found that I could be the best version of all four depending on what I was called to do. My Task part helps me when giving presentations or training as I set agendas, create systems, and get organized in advance. My Leader part is confident and in charge of the training, like a conductor in front of an orchestra. My People part is really good at reading the room, making conversation, listening to stories, and connecting with the participants. My Free Spirit part finds a way to have fun, be flexible when issues arise, and discover creative ways to teach my audience. She's also very good at last-minute problem-solving. I am not any one part. I am the sum of all my parts, and I appreciate them all.

Exercise 28: Clear the Path to Your Best Self

Molding yourself into your Best Self begins with identifying the parts that support your journey and quieting the voices that distract and discourage you. Anne Lamott , author of *Bird by Bird* (1994), shares a funny tip given to her by a therapist that describes noticing all the squeaky, irritating inner voices that interfere with our goals and imagining they're little mice we can put in a mason jar to quiet them. I liked her idea, so I built on it, taking it even further:

1. Recognize and name the negative inner parts (those squeaky mice). You can still imagine them as mice, but name them based on their personalities, such as Controller, Pleaser, Worrier, or Perfectionist. Giving names to your pesky parts gives you the power of Awareness and allows you to notice which ones are showing up with which challenges.

2. Take a few slow deep breaths, then defuse the inner parts in some way so that you take back control of your actions. You could put them in a mason jar as suggested, give them alternate chores to keep busy, or simply ask them to step back and allow your Best Self to drive.

3. Call forth your Best Self with all your most supportive characteristics—offerings of bold, courageous, and helpful thoughts. This is the step that's most valuable because it allows you to find your own inner team of supporters. Once you have those, you'll go from being on the defensive to being on the offensive.

Acceptance comes into this process as well. The journey will have ups and downs requiring steadfast determination and grit. Accept that the same actions that brought you to this point are not going to get you to a new place; you *will* have to make changes to see new results.

Have self-compassion for that old version of yourself who's fighting this process. Your parts are trying to protect you in some way. You don't necessarily have to crack the code of why and what from. Still, it's important to acknowledge that these parts, with all their complicated thoughts, are not evil. They just need to be understood so that you can get beyond the block and propel yourself into the future.

Remember your inner parts have something to tell you. Listen, and be open to their message.

CHAPTER 8
PRIORITIES, OUTCOMES, AND GOALS

People with goals succeed because they know where they're going.

—Earl Nightingale

Priorities, Outcomes, and Goals 143

- Priorities
- Outcomes and Goals
- Outcome Statements
- Strategies to Accelerate Your Goals

Wouldn't it be great to know where you're heading and to have focus and direction? If you look at what's important to you—your priorities—and formulate them into desired outcomes and goals, you'll have a path laid out ahead of you. Think of your desired outcomes like good health or a thriving business: they're the targets you're trying to reach, and you need specific ways to reach them. The more realistic and specific the goal, the easier it is to reach.

Priorities

We know there's a finite amount of time in a day, but we don't always feel like we have a grasp on how to get everything done. A major key to seeing results is setting priorities and focusing on them as we set about our day. If we're clear about what's important to us, it's easier to say no to distractions and yes to what we want.

The next key is to look at the number and level of difficulty of our priorities and how they fit into our lives. If we try to do too much, we probably won't do any singular thing effectively. There's a story about fitting rocks into a jar. To fit them all in, you must start with the big rocks, move your way down to the medium- and small-sized rocks, and then fill in the gaps with sand. If you start with the sand, you'll never fit the big rocks in. If you fill your limited-size jar with too many big rocks, the jar will break.

In this scenario, big rocks represent the important tasks, projects, or issues in our lives—our priorities. I don't like to have more than one or two big priorities on my agenda at any given time, for example, otherwise, everything feels urgent. If something is important enough, it can wait until next quarter. Approach each day with a quick review of your big, medium, and small priorities, until it becomes second nature. Then create a daily list of tasks with your priorities in mind.

> **Be sure to include self-care and fun as essential priorities, or your life will be out of balance.**

Let's walk through the Action Cycle together with one broad challenge I see frequently in my coaching practice and my own life. I struggle most when it comes to doing anything important for myself—my business tasks, strategic Planning, writing, administrative priorities, and even my health habits. I know I'm not the only one who struggles with this because my clients and colleagues, especially small business owners with families, have shared this same sentiment.

I'm aware I tend to do for others ahead of myself and neglect my own priorities. I also do things that are in my comfort zone over things I have to stop and think about. Over the last decade, I've consciously accepted the challenge to make better use of my time, placing my own needs at a higher priority level than in the past. My Mindset is clear and decisive: *Establish my priorities and focus on them. Set boundaries with others so that they know I have priorities and needs.*

After Assessing options of what I'd like to achieve each year, I select one or two larger goals or projects to focus on. I then start Planning to achieve each goal and tracking each Action to keep me motivated. After Completion of each phase or goal, I take time for Reflection on my progress, celebrate my accomplishments, and prepare for the next phase or goal. It never turns out as perfectly as I hope, but that's to be expected.

Many people grapple with achieving life balance. What is that, exactly? For some, the idea that their lives are in balance means they have equal time, money, or energy devoted to all areas of their lives. However, that may not be realistic. Are you seeking life balance or life harmony? Which do you need more?

My publisher, Jenn T. Grace, who's a single mother, mentioned she has four days a week when she has full responsibility for her son, so she chooses to do less work on those days. She has three days when she goes all-out to tackle her business tasks, usually putting in twelve-hour days. While this might seem out of balance, it actually feels harmonious to her. And it works. Her priority is spending time with her son, and this system allows her to be slower, calmer, and more present on the days she's with him.

Not all priorities are task-related. Relationships can have issues too: *My coworker is driving me crazy with his snide comments. My family isn't helping around the house. My spouse and I aren't on the same page about an important issue.* If we choose to neglect seeking solutions to these issues, our relationships will suffer and we will live with the consequences. The same strategies I offer for task-related struggles apply to relationship struggles as well. The tricky thing about relationship goals is understanding that we can't control other people, only ourselves. Focus on what you want for your relationship and what you can do about it—not just on what you want for yourself or what you want someone else to do.

Setting priorities and looking at how they all influence each other allows us to plan our lives with more intention and balance. Prioritizing our wants and needs while finding a harmonious balance takes time and practice with trial and error. For me, the keys have been Acceptance of responsibility for my own happiness, Assessing all the possible solutions (including asking for help), limiting the number of big goals I pursue at any given time (prioritizing), and creating a plan of Action. That takes time and Reflection. It's also essential to have and keep a positive Mindset from beginning to end: *It's up to me to make these things happen in a way that feels authentic so that I can be at ease!*

Exercise 29: Set Priorities

Now it's your turn. What priorities might you be focusing on? Three important categories that seem to be most neglected are steps toward self-care, personal growth, and long-term Planning. They can be particularly tricky to pay attention to but have the greatest payoff.

Make a list of the big, medium, and small priorities on your plate right now. Based on what you've listed, can you realistically accomplish any of these in the near future? Is there anything that can wait for a later date or be delegated to someone else?

Outcomes and Goals

When starting the goal-setting process, don't try to figure out "the how" just yet. Name "the what," which is your desired outcome. Our desired outcomes can stem from any number of reasons. Here are some examples:

- ❖ Fix a problem
- ❖ Complete a project
- ❖ Set a new course for your personal or professional life
- ❖ Pursue something new
- ❖ Make life easier, better, or more fulfilling
- ❖ Complete an obligation

Other desired outcomes are about making us feel different or improving a relationship. You may want to alter the course of an issue you're struggling with or make an intentional and proactive change that has the potential to change you in the process. Here are some possibilities:

- ❖ I want to:
  - ➢ feel comfortable retiring,
  - ➢ have a better relationship with (_),
  - ➢ feel more confident in my job/business,
  - ➢ feel organized,
  - ➢ be a better parent,
  - ➢ have life balance,
  - ➢ manage my stress, or
  - ➢ get back in the flow with my writing.

- ➢ Your top-level goal (desired outcome) might be to have genuine and respectful relationships at work and at home. What smaller goals would support that?

OUTCOME STATEMENTS

Let's revisit the concept of **outcome statements**—a declaration that states what you want to create at a high level. This time, I want you to add why this is important to you. Here's an example I used last year:

- ❖ My Outcome Statement: I am the person who manages my stress better and creates a better life balance. I want to have less stressful thoughts and more confident thoughts. My sanity, happiness, relationships, and life will improve.
- ❖ Why Now: My life is hectic. It's important that I go from a feeling that everything is in constant chaos to having a life with ease and flow.
- ❖ The Smaller Goals That Will Support This Outcome:
  - ➢ I will use my Positive Intelligence app every day to listen to stress-busting tips and help me reframe my thinking.
  - ➢ I will schedule three hours a week to meditate, be alone, or take walks.
  - ➢ I will create fun memories with my family and friends at least once per week.
  - ➢ I will journal so that I can acknowledge what I'm grateful for. (This goal is never really completed, but I can reflect monthly to assess my progress.)

As you begin to name important outcomes you want in your life, you'll begin to see that there are specific goals that will support that outcome. Think of them as the building blocks to get what you desire. Outcomes and their supporting goals are the vision you're working toward—your target. If you say your desired outcomes out loud, the universe will find ways to help you fulfill them.

- ❖ I want to see the world.
- ❖ I want to connect with people.
- ❖ I want to be a writer.
- ❖ I want to be a better leader at work and at home.

These sweeping goals are connected to your values, the bottom line of what's in your heart. Angela Duckworth's book *Grit* would call them "top-level" goals (Duckworth 2018). If asked why you have a goal and your answer is "Just because" or "I've always wanted to do it," try reframing it to "It's who I want to be."

Now let's look at broad goals with a more specific focus:

- ❖ I want to communicate better with my children so that they feel heard, supported, and loved.
- ❖ I want to be proud of my home and fix anything that's broken or needs attention.
- ❖ I want to grow my business by creating new products or offerings.

Goals serve an important purpose. They're like a compass or GPS giving us focus and direction. Without goals, we may wander aimlessly, never knowing whether we've reached our desired destination.

To expand on this idea, let's consider **SMART goals**, which stands for specific, measurable, attainable, realistic, and timely. The "R" can also stand for resonant, or something that's meaningful to you; it's not someone else's goal, it's yours. The "T" can also stand for thrilling! A true SMART goal isn't wishy-washy. It's something you can point to and say, "Yes, I did it" or "No, I didn't do it." An example might be, "I will send out a personal note card to a client, friend, or family member every week."

To create goals, our first task is to identify the thing(s) that will move us further toward a desired outcome. For instance, if you're on a journey to improve your health, your smaller goals might include losing ten pounds, eating more fruits and vegetables, exercising, and having an annual physical. To make them SMART, you answer how much, how often, and by when. Here are a few more examples of outcomes and SMART goals:

❖ Have a thriving business with ten existing clients and two new client consultations each month.
❖ File all papers and have a tidy desk at the end of each workday.
❖ Lead my team through one productive meeting each month. (Then define "productive" as a second goal.)

If one of your SMART goals is a little hard to measure, try making it more specific. When you write a goal in the SMART format, it's clear what you want to achieve, both for yourself and for others.

When I'm working with a new client, we often begin with top-level, broad, desired outcomes and then discuss what each would mean in their daily lives. We talk about the specific (SMART) goals they'll need to accomplish to feel like they're succeeding and why those particular goals are important to them, including why now.

Exercise 30: Write Your Outcome Statement and Goals

If you had to write down only one top-level goal to focus on for the next year, what would it be? In this theoretical game, you'll put on blinders once you decide, setting aside any other big goals for the future. Prioritize, then select just one. If you're excited to keep going, then you've probably hit the right desired outcome to focus on.

1. Write down your desired outcome: I want to [the outcome you desire] because [why it's important].
2. Answer the question, Why now?
3. List the possible SMART goals that will help you.
4. Answer the question, What type(s) of maintenance will this outcome require once completed?

Goals about Feelings

Not all goals can be written in the SMART format, particularly if they're based on emotion. If that's the case, they're more likely to be a top-level outcome, and you'll have to think of clever, smaller steps to get there. For example, if you say, "I want to feel more confident," what specifically do you want to feel confident doing or saying? In what situations? What activities can build your confidence?

Confidence is more often a quality tied to a specific situation or task; you may not feel it at other times. The more you do something, the more your confidence grows. Experts in public speaking might say, "Fake it till you make it, and practice, practice, practice." Do you want more confidence speaking in front of an audience or at a team meeting? What are three potential steps to get you there gradually? Who might support you?

Exercise 31: Explore Your Emotional Goals

1. To make a lasting change, it helps to name your starting point with an intimate level of Awareness. Ask yourself these questions that will help you point out the goals you want to add to your list:

   → What is at the core of this current struggle? How does it make me feel?

   → How do I want to feel? (That becomes the goal to explore.)

   → What habits and routine behaviors are ingrained in this situation?

   → What behaviors are currently happening that ideally won't be happening in the future?

   → If I were to reach this new outcome, what would I be thinking, feeling, and doing differently every day? Who would I become?

2. Name your desired outcome(s), answer why now, and list the goals that could help you achieve the outcome(s).

3. What could help you maintain this new outcome?

Goal-Setting Spectrum

As a practice, goal setting lives on a spectrum. Some people swear by setting goals and others avoid them completely. In an ideal world, we have daily, weekly, monthly, and yearly goals that give us focus and direction. We may even create five-year plans and modify them after each annual Reflection. We break our goals down into smaller steps and track our progress regularly.

On either side of this ideal are wide variations—those who avoid goals and those who obsess about them. Goal Avoiders may feel too constricted, thinking they have to give up something or feeling it's too hard for them. They might even feel triggered every time the word is mentioned. Goal Obsessors may exert so much time and energy thinking about achieving their goals that they forget to enjoy their journeys and celebrate their wins. They put unnecessary stress on themselves and let their Achilles heels—the Hyper-Achiever, Competitor, or Stickler—run the show. Here are some other parts that often show up when we're trying to set goals, along with their typical behaviors:

- ❖ **Goal Avoiders** have an aversion to setting goals and might even fear them due to past experiences of perceived failure.
- ❖ **Fire Extinguishers** have one particular goal—putting out fires. They haven't realized the value and return on investment that goals and strategies can provide.
- ❖ **Inconsistent Goal Setters** shoot for some goals, give up on others, and lack a system.
- ❖ **Goal Embracers** set very specific and measurable goals with steps that are attainable and realistic, using them as guidelines for their time and energy.

- ❖ **Goal Obsessors** focus so much on goals that they can't enjoy the journey. They put too much weight on achieving one hundred percent and don't celebrate their partial wins.

In my experience, Goal Embracers are the ideal, and I've come to realize that even they can be on a continuum. Some focus on immediate or short-term goals, while others include time for Planning mid-range and long-term goals. There are also those who set goals only at work or at home, and those who are more holistic and include goals in all areas of their lives. Goal Embracers also tend to embrace routines, strategies, and processes, giving them added tools for time management.

Wherever you're on the goal continuum, I hope you'll look for a holistic approach that keeps your life in harmony. All work and no play will make anyone a stressed-out mess! By both achieving your goals and consciously adding time for fun and relaxation, you get to decide what could make your life a little better or a little more joyful.

Exercise 32: Identify Your Goal Patterns

You might be good at identifying, setting, and achieving some goals and struggle with others. Let's explore these questions to grow more of your Awareness around goals. Once you see the pattern, it might help you embrace and achieve the next goal, even if it seems difficult.

1. Successes

   → Which types of goals do you typically accomplish?
   → Why do you think that's the case?
   → Are your skills and confidence level a good match to the requirements for reaching the goal?
   → What thoughts that support your successes might be missing when you're struggling?

2. Challenges

   → Which goals are the hardest for you to accomplish or feel so difficult that you don't bother trying?
   → What circumstances or distractions are most challenging?
   → What thoughts tend to get in the way of your success?

Exploring these questions helps raise your Awareness to see patterns. You might have some limiting beliefs about certain goals, circumstances, and relationships as well as money, food, life balance, or time management that are keeping you stuck: *Will this be hard, take too much of my time, or require me to give up things I love?* That internal line of questioning creates a Mindset that may cause you to avoid dealing with the issue because you're already focusing on the problem.

What would your internal questions be like if you were to focus on the outcome and the opportunity?

- ❖ What is important right now?
- ❖ What is possible if I achieve this goal?
- ❖ How great will it feel to complete this project?
- ❖ How will my life be different?

Strategies to Accelerate Your Goals

Three key strategies can help us accelerate the accomplishment of our goals: solve the issue once, ease into big goals, and embrace the work. To solve an issue once, pause and review the issue, then ease into the long-term solution to improve the situation. For example, if one of the challenges you want to overcome is an ongoing, chronic problem, it might be helpful to frame it differently. Rather than struggling through this one situation, it might make more sense to address the bigger struggle so that you don't have the same recurring problem. "I want to get through this next batch of reports" becomes "I want to find a new system to make this easier" or "I want to manage my time better so I'm not rushing to get things done." Find a broader strategy that will solve your long-term issue. These strategies typically include a system, process, checklist, or routine that's easy to repeat over and over.

Take time to make time—develop a strategy!

An executive coach I know typically spends three hours interviewing new clients and another eight hours writing comprehensive reports based on the assessment results and the interviews. That process is very labor intensive, and the agency doesn't pay for all that time. The coach can choose to either work extra hours at night or on weekends to keep up or find a better process that takes less time and provides similar results. The goal might be to "Create a strategy, system, and/or template that would allow me to complete the intake process in less time." A little time spent now will save hours of time later.

One of my first clients was a dancer and choreographer who also taught at a university. One situation that was creating a chronic problem for her was recovering from frequent but necessary travel on the weekends. She dreaded Sunday nights because she struggled to unpack, eat a healthy meal, and prepare for early Monday appointments. Her obstacles appeared to be fatigue and procrastination. After a coaching session, she developed the "Unpack the Suitcase Strategy": before she ever left home, she would prepare by having a meal ready for Sunday night and keeping her Monday mornings appointment-free whenever possible. Using this strategy, she was able to settle in on Sunday nights and eat a healthy meal, and she no longer felt the dread of what she might face on Monday.

When you identify an issue and take a good look at it, you have the opportunity to uncover what needs to be solved. Before being strategic, my client judged herself for procrastinating or being lazy. After creating a strategy, she realized she was judging herself too harshly and saw the value of strategizing and Planning. Take a deeper look at your situation and ask yourself the right questions to find your solution.

Create a strategy to make a chronic problem a little bit easier to handle.

Easing In

A strategy to successfully tackle large goals is something I call **Easing In**: taking a gradual approach with a longer timeline. If you've had a bucket-list goal for a long time, chances are it feels big and/or scary. Easing In allows you to take the bigness of it and break it down into chunks. Ask yourself, *What is one step I could start with?* Give your brain some time to find the solutions for you. Easing In also allows you to make the goal less scary. As you take baby steps, you'll build confidence in your abilities and belief that the goal is achievable.

A compelling, long-term goal that can simultaneously inspire us and scare us is the kind we tend to defer to the future, and often that future never comes. One term used to describe this type of goal is a **Big Hairy Audacious Goal** (BHAG), first coined in 1994 by authors Jim Collins and Jerry Porras (2004) in their book *Built to Last: Successful Habits of Visionary Companies*.

Not all goals are BHAGs, but if you're stalling or stuck in neutral and not taking Action, your mind is considering it one. In this case, lean into the idea that even the scariest goals can be accomplished if you put in the time, effort, and Planning; seek support when necessary; and keep a positive Mindset. Use the Action Cycle! Here are some examples of BHAGs:

- ❖ I will quit my job and start a business I am passionate about.
- ❖ I will give up processed food.
- ❖ I will do (__) for the first time.

After you identify any BHAG, you can clarify it, brainstorm a list of steps to accomplish it, and identify its potential challenges, all while increasing your Awareness. Then, start Assessing your options, find an empowered Mindset, and turn your Planning into Action. A really large goal will likely need phases that incorporate many steps. Each phase could take months or even years to achieve. Examples that come to mind include becoming a doctor, starting a business, or doing a large renovation of your home. To get there, remember why this goal is important to you. Doing so is like having headlights in a fog and gas in your tank: it allows you to see where you're going and propels you forward.

Let's explore the goal of "I will declutter my whole house and keep it that way." I'll admit, this sounds like a BHAG because I said, "My whole house." If I dare add that it will be "hard" and "take a long time," it will increase the likelihood that I won't tackle it. The all-or-nothing approach and hard Mindset will cause me to avoid, delay, or give up on my goal. The pain seems to outweigh the benefits. Or does it? At some point, I might get fed up with being stuck in the same predicament and feel inspired to take Action. My thinking would then shift from *I can't do it* to *This is worth the effort*. Using the Easing In strategy, I start by asking myself what the first step to this big goal might be that might only take ten minutes. I can start with filing papers on my desk, filling one bag a week for Goodwill, or cataloging what's in every box in the attic. By breaking it down and easing your way in, you might realize that a goal is less difficult than you thought.

Exercise 33: Ease In

Imagine a goal that would benefit from Easing In.

1. Name the goal.
2. Name your current Mindset and how you want to feel.
3. Write down a few first steps that you could do now to ease into your goal.
4. What might you do if improving relationships is your goal?
5. If better health is your goal, where might you begin? What's one healthy step you could take today?

The more you struggle, delay, or defer a goal to the future, the more you may want to simplify it so that it's not such a huge leap at first. Once you've built up some success and your confidence is higher, you can stretch toward bigger steps that will accelerate your goal even further. Confidence is like a muscle—it will atrophy if you don't use it, but it will get stronger when you do.

Embrace the Work

Lamott's book *Bird by Bird* reminded me of another very important strategy: to accomplish a goal, we have to embrace doing the work. To get healthier, for example, we need to think, act, and eat like a healthy person, embracing a new relationship with food and exercise. Most people who lose weight will gain it back because they haven't really changed inside. They've played a temporary game and slipped back into their old habits. (I can relate!)

To be a good leader, you must embrace both who you are right now (strengths and flaws) and who you want to be. You need to embody the skills, thoughts, and actions of the type of leader you want to be.

To become a published author, you need to embrace writing. That involves spending time with a pen and paper (or your keyboard) and getting through shitty first drafts in order to get to the gems that will eventually become your final work. Don't get too far ahead of yourself worrying about finding an agent or publisher until you've mastered the discipline of writing—and write often.

Becoming a successful service-based entrepreneur gives us a little more complicated situation because it requires being good at something and doing that work while also working on your business. There are two different goals to focus on: Planning your business steps and then taking Action. Perhaps create a niche, an intake process, a website, a signature presentation, a social media campaign, and/or a newsletter. Taking Action sometimes requires you to take steps you don't love but your goal requires. You might need to put yourself out there and ask people to be your clients. You can't just slap up a website and hope that people will find you. If you don't know about marketing or website building, you may also need to ask for help or hire a professional.

Each of these examples have something in common: they are goals that take time, require consistent behavior, and need maintenance—a subject I'll cover next. This means they require new habits and systems to perpetuate the progress before, during, and after the initial goal is achieved. In other words, you must become a new version of you to accomplish the goal.

Exercise 34: Embrace the Person You're Becoming

When it comes to your main goal, what will it require to take all the steps you've planned out? Who will you be when you achieve your goal? What thoughts will keep you moving forward? Continue to ask yourself the following questions, and you'll continue to grow:

1. Am I embracing the person I want to be most? (What Action am I taking?)
2. Am I living intentionally and with commitment, one step at a time?
3. What thoughts support me in this goal?

Goals Require Maintenance

The last strategy I want to emphasize is embracing the maintenance phase of any goal. There are many goals that, once completed, require maintenance. Organizing a desk, restructuring a business, or getting a job are just a few goals that, once completed, will require maintenance. There are many routes to completing the goal, but once achieved you might need to define "maintenance" as a whole new goal with a brand-new plan of Action.

Let me share my experience dealing with weight loss and be honest with my results. My desired outcome was to get healthy, with a focused goal of losing weight.

In the summer of 2012, I decided I was going to lose forty pounds by the end of that year. I had many reasons. My joints were hurting, my clothes didn't fit, and I felt much older than my actual fifty-five years. Over the summer I'd been easing into the *I will do it* Mindset by joining a women-only gym. I had also worked with a nutritionist and learned that although wheat and corn were a substantial portion of my diet, they were causing inflammation. I made little shifts and lost a few pounds in two months—not a stellar result.

Then something changed as though a switch had been flipped. I connected with a coaching friend of mine named Bonnie, who had used a very specific method to lose weight. It focused on smaller meals, limiting sugar, and encouraged one larger "lean and green" meal per day. I learned to plan my meals and eat only what was written in my plan. The clarity of the plan, the accountability from Bonnie, and the fact that the plan matched my preference for smaller meals throughout the day made it seem relatively easy to follow.

I talked with Bonnie weekly and tried new recipes. I made a 100 percent commitment for a relatively short period of four months and boosted my commitment by focusing on my why. I wanted to look and feel healthier while releasing the joint pain. With every Action, even baby steps, my commitment to the plan and belief in myself grew. I was excited and motivated to see the results happen right before my eyes. I even lost weight through Halloween, Thanksgiving, and Christmas thanks to the routines I had developed. I lost forty pounds in four months and felt great!

There were four phases to my success and a thought pattern that went with each:

1. Doubtful: *How can I accomplish this? I'll fall off the wagon in the first week! It's too hard.*
2. Decisive: *I absolutely will do this.* (This decisiveness came after I had a clear plan.)
3. Action-Oriented: *Each day is clear; I will plan my food ahead of time, shop wisely, stick with the plan, and celebrate my success one small step at a time with pride.*
4. Completion-Focused: *I won't stop till I reach my goal.*

By December 31, 2012, I looked and felt wonderful. I even celebrated with a new wardrobe.

What do you think happened next? Let's hear from a few experts on weight management before you chime in with your guesses:

- ❖ In reference to increasing your appetite and slowing down your metabolism, Scott Kahan, MD and director of the National Center for Weight and Wellness at George Washington University in Washington, DC, notes, "Your body fights against the long-term maintenance of that weight" (Goodman 2016).
- ❖ "Food is harder to kick than crack cocaine," says Dr. Susan Peirce Thompson, bestselling author of Bright Line Eating: The Science of Living Happy, Thin, & Free. "Among the obese who try to lose weight,

the failure rate is 99 percent. Literally. Ninety-nine percent do not succeed at getting slim. And for the precious one percent who do succeed, the triumph is temporary" (Thompson 2017, 2).

After struggling with addictions to both drugs and food, Dr. Pierce Thompson was able to overcome her drug addiction, but it took much longer to be free of her addiction to sugar and flour, even after getting her PhD in brain and cognitive sciences. Her book is the story of her abstinence, the science behind food addiction, and the steps to her Bright Line Eating program.

As you may have guessed, my triumph was temporary. It took almost ten years, but I gained much of my forty pounds back. As we all know, I am not alone in my experience. What I didn't do successfully was a full Reflection step, nor did I create a plan of maintenance to stick with after I reached my goal. My "100 percent commitment" ended after my four-month process. I also didn't realize how addicted I was to sugar. I had succumbed to old habits and let my guard down. The sugar addiction came back with a vengeance, and I rationalized my weight gain: *It's just a few pounds.*

As my willpower slipped, my Mindset shifted. Over time, I lost the motivation and enthusiasm of my Committer part. My Rationalizer figured, *I lost forty pounds once, so how hard can it be to do it again?* That's also the part that chimes in after a good workout: *Now you can eat more and still lose weight!*

I'd like to blame my final weight gain on COVID-19 when almost everyone's Indulger and Victim were triggered, but the reality is that I have to own it myself. I lived in leggings with stretch waistbands and ate whatever I wanted. Boy, did I have a rude awakening in 2021 when I put on zippered jeans and warm-weather clothes! Since then I've stopped gaining weight and have put my health back in the priority column.

For some goals, Completion doesn't always mean complete. With goals that require post-completion maintenance, I suggest you immediately set a new goal to keep things going, perhaps even before you reach the finish line. I encourage you to be mindful and specific. Your plan may look similar to the last phase of your original goal, but it might be totally different. Lay out the what and the how, adjust your Mindset to keep it going, and use the Action Cycle to assist you.

Exercise 35: Maintain Your Goals

1. Name a goal that would take some effort to maintain once achieved.
2. Why do you want to maintain this?
3. What daily, weekly, or monthly steps would it take to maintain this new achievement?
4. What Mindset and thoughts would help you stay on course?
5. What new process, tracking system, or method of accountability would help you?
6. Describe how your identity has changed / will change with this maintained goal.

PART THREE
Take Eight Steps

Life is a cycle of ends and starts.
—Mark Webber

THE EIGHT STEPS OF THE ACTION CYCLE:

1 Awareness	2 Acceptance	3 Mindset	4 Assessing
5 Planning	6 Action	7 Completion	8 Reflection

Ten years ago, when Anna Cole and I co-created the "Five A Change Process," we wanted to help our clients work their way from Awareness to Action. Since that time, I've modified the process to add three more steps that are crucial to the cycle: Mindset, Completion, and Reflection. Mindset is at the core because our thoughts drive our ability to take Action. The last two steps, Completion and Reflection, give us the strategies to finish a project all the way and then reflect on our results so that we celebrate, learn from the process, and find our next steps forward.

By this point in the book, I hope you've already been growing your Awareness, the first big step in the Action Cycle. You've identified some of your innate wiring, challenged some of your limiting beliefs, and discovered and named some of your inner parts that are on this journey with you. You also have a better sense of what Mindset will help you shift into decisiveness. Chances are, you've also selected goals and started to work on them.

What I offer you now is an even deeper look into the eight steps of the Action Cycle, giving you a greater chance to go from doubtful to decisive and take the Action you desire. All you need now is to identify the issue you want to solve and move forward using the eight steps in the Action Cycle. Repeat this part of the book over and over again with each new issue or goal that you wish to tackle. You can do it!

STEP 1
AWARENESS

> *Self-awareness involves deep personal honesty.*
> *It comes from asking and answering hard questions.*
>
> —Stephen Covey

Awareness is the first step. It's when you identify the situation you're in and explore what's making you feel doubtful, stuck, or frustrated. You're at the starting gate with a Mindset that has you feeling stuck and frustrated and with an issue or a goal you're chomping at the bit to resolve. Whether the goal is for your personal or professional life or the issue is little or big, there's something you want to feel better about. You might want more of something or less of something, or you might want to fix something that's not working (literally or figuratively), start a new habit, or make a big change. Once this Awareness is at the forefront of your mind, you have the opportunity to address it.

If you stuff down and avoid the issue, there will always be something that brings it back up, often at an inopportune time. Addressing an issue doesn't always mean you have to *do* something. It might mean that you'll *stop* doing something, such as pleasing, avoiding, or rescuing. You might let go of the need for control or decide that it's better not to do that project until next year. At least you'll have made a decision.

I exhibited at an event recently where I asked people what they were feeling stuck on or doubtful about. The topics they mentioned revealed their deepest desires to change careers, retire, get healthy, grow their business, manage change, address family issues, improve their finances, and get published. What do those issues all have in common? They aren't urgent. No one is knocking on the door waiting for them to make a decision or get into Action. They aren't accountable to anyone but themselves. According to Tim Urban's TED Talk "Inside the Mind of a Master Procrastinator," there is no scary internal "Panic Monster" telling us to hurry up (Urban 2016). Those voices are "when you get around to it" goals that are claiming real estate in our brains and making us miserable, but not miserable enough or confident enough to act upon.

When you become aware that you feel stuck or doubtful, that's the time to put this issue on your priority list if you want to have peace of mind and feel accomplished. If you don't, it will still be an issue for you a month, a year, or even a decade from now. It's not a matter of how soon you want to address it, it's a matter of having the right tools and strategies to address it.

These are just a few of the questions you might ask yourself to gain clarity:

- What's going on? What problem or issue do you want to address?
- How does it make you feel?
- What do you want instead?
- Why is this important?
- How have your wiring, experiences, or inner parts influenced this current issue?
- What thoughts are you having about this issue (what is your current Mindset)?

Next, become more aware of why this issue is important and what you already have to help you solve it, including your strengths, passions, and resources. Ask yourself what's working and not working for you. Most importantly, ask yourself, *What do I want?* Take the time to dream about it. Journals are really helpful at this step. Someone contemplating a career change might ask themselves, *What do I love and not love about my current job? What makes me feel unsettled? When is my energy high, and when do I feel drained? How much stress does change cause for me and when? Why is it important to address this now?*

Awareness is the first step to making any positive change in your life.

The point of the Awareness step of the Action Cycle is to gather information and evaluate your thoughts and emotions while gaining clarity. You name the issue, name your starting point, and begin to dream about what you want. You're at Point A, and you want to get to Point B. This goes back to all the reasons we set goals: to fix a problem, to pursue a dream, or to create a better system for our lives. To get there, you need to recognize all the influences and variables that will affect your ability to make that happen.

The Author

An author was working on her book and had committed to writing at least three or four times a week. She was writing a memoir about her life experience and her struggle for self-actualization. As she grew closer and closer to finishing the book, she noticed she was slowing down. Every little distraction was keeping her from writing. She had lost her all-or-nothing commitment.

As she explored Awareness, she noted two reasons why she had slowed down. The main reason seemed to be that she was avoiding the *What next?* question. Once she was done writing her manuscript, she'd have to start the expensive and scary process of hiring an editor and publisher to "birth" her book. If she dawdled, she wouldn't have to address these issues. The second thing she realized was that some memories were very fuzzy, and she felt guilty for not remembering things.

Awareness becomes an opportunity to address obstacles with a rational and honest frame of mind rather than a reactive one. Once the author knew the reasons for her hesitation, she reframed her thinking. The energy and commitment to finish her book returned.

The next step after Awareness is Acceptance, when you decide to do something about the issue you identified. In the author's case, she accepted that it was important to recommit to finishing her book. To do that, she committed to the investment and found people to flesh out her memories. She told herself, *We can't always remember everything, and it's okay to ask for help* (two very helpful Mindsets). Sometimes Awareness reveals that we are conflating two or three issues into one. When we pull them apart and name them, we can start to address them separately and stop procrastinating.

Exercise 36: Raise Your Awareness

General Questions to Raise Your Awareness

1. What do you want, what are your goals, and what do you need? Stay mindful of the emotions that will direct you toward these answers.
2. What makes you tick? Keep in mind your personality type and inner parts.
3. What is on your mind that's troubling you about your current circumstances?

Understanding More About YOU

4. What drains you or triggers you to feel overwhelmed, doubtful, and avoidant?
5. What habits do you have that support and/or hurt you?
6. What do you value, what is important to you, and what excites you?"
7. What strengths do you have, what are you proud of, and what are you grateful for?
8. What do you tend to focus on? The urgent? The past, the future, or the present? The unknown?

Understanding the Situation

9. What specifically do you want, and why is it important?
10. What is here now that wouldn't be here if the issue were solved?

- ❖ Outside influences and obstacles (other people, situations)
- ❖ Daily experiences
- ❖ Internal feelings and thoughts

11. What have you done about the issue so far?
12. What might you need as far as research, information, cost/benefit analysis?

Current Me Questions

13. How does the Current Me typically address this type of issue?
14. What Achilles heels, such as habits or weaknesses, get in my way?
15. What parts of me hold me back? (For example, Avoider, Perfectionist, or Analyzer.)

Best Self Questions

16. How do I imagine my Best Self taking care of this issue?
17. What strengths do I have that can help me?
18. What parts of me can help if I focus on growing them? (For example, Curiosity or Leader.)
19. What lasting traits would I want my Best Self to have?

STEP 2
ACCEPTANCE

> *God, grant me the serenity to accept the things I cannot change, the courage to change the things I can, and the wisdom to know the difference.*
>
> —Reinhold Niebuhr, The Serenity Prayer

When you're struggling with something and are aware that you're going around in circles or avoiding the topic altogether, **Acceptance** is the first path out. Most importantly, accept the things you cannot change, including people (yourself and others). Accept responsibility for achieving your goal, and remember that you can take charge instead of waiting or hoping for something to change.

Acceptance Statements:

- *Now, not later, is the time to do something about this issue.*
- *I am responsible for my own happiness. My future begins with me.*
- *I accept things, situations, other people, and myself.*
- *I accept reality, and I'll make it work.*
- *Negative thinking will only slow me down.*
- *I can decide what I want first and figure out how later.*
- *It takes time and thought to move forward, and I will do it.*

> Many years ago, I was stuck in the middle of two challenging projects. I had a sense of responsibility to complete them and was determined to do so. One was a business presentation that could lead to a book, and the other was a big project for a volunteer role. I was aware that I was avoiding both projects and getting behind on their timelines. I was feeling overwhelmed, convinced I had taken on too much.
>
> After days of doing next to nothing, I took time to pause and ask myself what the heck I was waiting for. Like snapping out of a daydream, I

realized that I was committed to both of these projects, I was perfectly capable of executing them, and it was time to get moving! No more avoidance, complaints, or wishing they were magically solved.

I decided to start by moving one of the projects forward. It really didn't matter which one, as long as I did something! I was able to shift into high gear, picking a project—a first step—and a very quick deadline to complete it. I felt so relieved when that one step was done. It was like a cork had been released from a champagne bottle.

The next morning, I woke up with my brain on fire! I had so many ideas for the other project that I ran to my office and started filling out index cards. By releasing the worry and feelings of doubt, I had allowed my brain to get back to work.

We all go through times of stagnation or feeling stuck at a crossroads: *Do I work on this or that? Do I finally address this thing now or wait until a later date?* The more time we spend in a negative spiral, the heavier the issue feels and the more likely we are to avoid or delay addressing it. The trick to shifting your thinking toward an actual solution is to accept the challenge by addressing it now. Know that there's always something within your control that you can do to improve your life, your work, or your circumstances. Accept that it starts with you.

In Acceptance, there's an active taking in what you accept and an active deflection or letting go of the things that get in your way. Challenge any limiting beliefs that are undermining your ability to act. Limiting beliefs can begin as, *I could never* and *We have to*. Turn those around and accept what's truly possible.

For now, you have certain skills, circumstances, challenges, and events happening in your life. Accepting yourself, others, and your circumstances will allow you to move forward. You can still influence change, but Acceptance is a necessary starting point to break you out of the *shoulda, coulda, woulda,* or *if only* Mindsets. Acceptance puts you in charge.

If you have a broken car and accept that you need to do something about it, you could consider one of the following: ask the mechanic whether it's worth fixing, look at your finances to see whether you can afford a new or used car, or explore other options to take care of your needs. If your business is slow, you can accept that what you're doing right now isn't working well enough and that it's time to make changes. If your health is in jeopardy, your relationships are full of tension, or your life is too chaotic, you can deny it, ignore it, or avoid it, or you can accept that you *will* do something about it.

In another version of the two-project story, a client of mine prepped for her coach certification exam before having surgery rather than pushing her big business goal to grow new clients. Though she wanted to do both, she settled on the one that was more realistic and kept her feeling active. She accepted that it was better for her to do a good job on one than a poor job on two. She recovered from surgery, passed her exam, and is now focusing on growing her business.

If you're facing any project and feeling stuck—writing, organizing, moving, or project management at work—Acceptance is about commitment to the project. Accept that you *will* make it a priority, face the obstacles head-on, and make it happen. You don't have to know how yet, just start with Acceptance. Breathe it in. Sit with it. Know that if you want to mold your life in any way, Acceptance is the doorway to that change.

Exercise 37: Practice Acceptance (with Reframes)

Read the following questions and reframes and select two that represent your biggest struggle. Perhaps a part of you answered the question with an emphatic "No!" Your challenge now is to repeatedly read the reframes (in italics), until they become part of your automatic thinking. You can also write your own reframes. This will help you develop a new super-highway of Acceptance.

1. Do you accept that now is the time to address this issue? → *If not now, why not, and when?*
2. Do you accept responsibility for your own happiness? → *I own my happiness. I accept it's up to me.*
3. Do you accept yourself for who you are right now, flaws and all? → *No one is perfect, and we all have room for improvement!*
4. Do you accept others for who they are? → *I know that I can't change other people, and I don't have control over them.*
5. Do you accept your current reality? → *I can change my circumstances if I do the work.*
6. Do you accept that negative thinking will only slow you down? → *I will consciously add positive thoughts to my day.*
7. Do you accept that you can decide what you want first, then decide how to do it later? → *I can, and I will figure it out with the rest of the Action Cycle steps.*

8. Do you accept that it takes time to see results? → *Small daily steps will make small shifts at first and large results later.*
9. Do you accept the challenge to do this work? → *I will pause to make conscious choices and commit to regaining control of my life. I will make the time.*

**State what is here.
State what you want.
Accept that it is in your best interest and ability to do something about it.**

STEP 3
MINDSET

> *If you don't like something, change it. If you can't change it, change your attitude.*
>
> —Maya Angelou

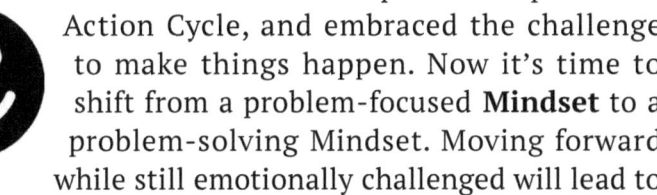

You've identified an issue to work on, worked through the Awareness and Acceptance steps of the Action Cycle, and embraced the challenge to make things happen. Now it's time to shift from a problem-focused **Mindset** to a problem-solving Mindset. Moving forward while still emotionally challenged will lead to less-than-stellar results, so breathe and put yourself back in neutral. No matter what you're feeling, pause, breathe, and accept that you're here to live your Best Life. You can do it. You can find the answers to this challenge.

As we saw in the last step, Acceptance is the first shift into a more positive way of looking at your challenge, issue, problem, or goal. It's the point where you commit to getting out of being stuck and into Action. Now it's time to zero in on your Mindset and continue through the Action Cycle in its entirety. Each of the reframes in the Acceptance exercise were new Mindsets.

Defining *Mindset* is a little tricky, as there seem to be many interpretations of the word. I like to think of our Mindset as the way we perceive our world and the lens through which we view our options. If you could summarize how you feel about an issue into just one phrase or sentence, that would probably be your Mindset. Other words for Mindset might be "perspective," "outlook," or "attitude."

Here are some examples of a positive Mindset:

- ❖ *I can do this, one step at a time.*
- ❖ *No time like the present; no day like today.*
- ❖ *Progress, not perfection.*

Merriam-Webster's Dictionary defines Mindset as "a mental attitude or inclination." Your Mindset is a reflection of your thoughts. Think of them as if on a dial from negative to neutral to positive, just like our Judge-O-Meter. Negative thoughts only reinforce problems or adverse outcomes that you're already worried about. Don't believe everything you think. Negative thoughts could be true or made up, but neutral thoughts maintain you, and positive thoughts are supportive, encouraging, and optimistic.

Your Mindset can shift from day to day and even hour by hour. It depends on what's going on around you, what your inner thoughts are, and how you interpret life's challenges. If you're very confident about your abilities in one area of your life while very insecure in another area, your Mindset is likely to have a similar swing from confident to doubtful.

I find great examples of Mindsets in the local news. "Failure is okay, keep striving for greatness," said Jesse Green, artist and motivational speaker for elementary school children (Martinez 2022). "I'm going to do this rehearsal and hope for the best. If it's not great, that's okay," said Unity Phelan, principal dancer in the New York City Ballet (Kourlas 2022). One of my clients shared her intentions and revealed her Mindset at the end of a coaching session: "I'm going to figure out all my options and then pick one. It's okay to explore."

All these examples reveal ways of making life an easier mental journey by using a frame of mind that promotes moving forward when life deals you a difficult hand. If you want to put the battle of doubt and decisiveness in your rearview mirror, you must choose an empowering Mindset. This begs the question, Can you choose a Mindset? I believe you can. By consciously choosing how you want to think about an issue rather than reacting to the circumstances, you give yourself a new advantage.

Rather than sitting in doubt or beating yourself up, focus on what's going well, what's possible, and what you want. Doing so allows your mind to open to all possibilities, which is the fourth step in the Action Cycle—Assessing your options. Thoughts become your Mindset, so use them wisely.

Here are four examples of a positive Mindset for life and how they can shift your focus:

1. *Progress, not perfection.* → Activities that maximize progress
2. *One step at a time.* → One small step, and then another, etc.
3. *What is my ONE thing today?* → The one project or step I will focus on today
4. *This is important to me.* → Priorities

Converting Challenges

> *Any issue or challenge can be converted into a gift or an opportunity.*
>
> —Shirzad Chamine

In this quote from *Positive Intelligence*, Chamine reminds us to reframe our thoughts and find a new Mindset. I call this strategy "converting challenges." A poor interview becomes an opportunity to grow. A lost client gives you room to take on a new project. The COVID-19 shutdown gave everyone an opportunity to learn new technology and new ways to stay connected with loved ones. I'm still using Discord, a communication app, to share Wordle results daily with four of my sisters.

To examine your converted challenges, start by asking yourself, *When did a challenge or "failure" become an opportunity for me to learn or grow?* Your Mindset can guide you to look for the gift and/or the opportunity no matter what challenge you're facing. If you reflect on any wins in your past, you might find a new Mindset that will help in this current challenge. Your Mindset is your opportunity to effectively deal with life, love, work, finances, home projects, friends, family, personal growth, or any other issue—every day.

You can also convert insight into a new Mindset. For example, *I know I work better with a partner* becomes *I don't have to do this alone*. Here's what I do when I'm struggling with a project that's meaningful to me but feels hard:

1. I focus on my why—the reason I want something.
2. I remember that I'm creative, resourceful, and whole, some of the cornerstones of professional coaching.
3. I remind myself that *I can figure it out* and that *Doing the work is worth it*.

As we know from previous chapters, declaring a Mindset is like choosing what gear you want to be in: reverse, neutral, or drive.

- ❖ *With my family helping me, I can accomplish anything!*
- ❖ *I don't have to have it all figured out before I get started. I'll begin with Step 1.*
- ❖ *If my mind begins to stray, my intentional focus will bring me back to today's plan over and over again.*

Win the Battle, Set the Mood

> *I have come to a frightening conclusion. I am the decisive element in the classroom. It is my personal approach that creates the climate. It is my daily mood that makes the weather. As a teacher I possess a tremendous power to make a child's life miserable or joyous. I can be a tool of torture or an instrument of inspiration. I can humiliate or humor, hurt or heal. In all situations, it is my response that decides whether a crisis will be escalated or de-escalated, and a child humanized or de-humanized.*
>
> —Haim G. Ginott, *Teacher and Child: A Book for Parents and Teachers*

This quote from Ginott has been one of my favorite quotes for years, though the version I knew didn't have the references to the teacher-child relationship. These words spoke to me. "I am the decisive element ... my approach creates the climate ... my mood creates the weather ... I can humiliate or humor, hurt or heal." I'm a metaphor junkie, which is why I've asked you to think of the weather as a reflection of your Mindset, your disposition. When you're struggling or doubtful, your thoughts are like a battleground—doubtful versus decisive, fearful versus courageous. The emotions and feelings that win out are ultimately up to you. In a tough situation, are you bright skies or thunderstorms? Do you have constant road detours due to flooding or hurricane winds? Perhaps your sunny skies help you see all the options and calm those around you.

Because you're a traveler heading toward your goal, it's crucial to keep yourself in the present, be observant along your route, and have a realistic, sunny disposition. Negative Mindsets will cloud your vision and cause you many detours, or even end your travels. Positive Mindsets will illuminate your path, keep you in forward gear, and motivate you to take each step. Awareness and acknowledgment that obstacles *will* be coming helps you set your expectations properly, allowing you to be ready when they come your way.

> **You can't be decisive without a positive, confident, and empowering Mindset.**

You probably know whether you're an optimist who can't help but see the possibilities or a pessimist who has trouble seeing beyond potential problems. Studies have shown that we're typically wired one way or the other from a young age. However, science has also proven that we can actually rewire our brains to become more optimistic. As you make choices every minute of your day, be mindful of the weather you're creating for yourself. Even an optimist like me can have pessimistic or negative thoughts. I just choose not to dwell on them—I don't stay in the rainstorm. I acknowledge the thoughts for what they're trying to tell me and then switch the channel to one of my choosing.

Ways to Select an Empowered Mindset

When I went through my coach training at the Co-Active Training Institute, I learned a wonderful exercise called the

Perspective Wheel. The point of the exercise is to see that when we're struggling with an issue, it's probably because we're looking at it through a negative lens, perspective, or Mindset. If I'm feeling negative—confused, angry, helpless—then I know I need to shift my thinking to something more positive. You can try out more than one perspective to see what's most helpful. I usually go through three or four before I find the right Mindset, which is often a combination of my two favorites. It may help to get up and move around the room or sit in different seats at a table to really see a new perspective.

- ❖ The Mindset *I can't do all this in time!* results in feeling anxious and your brain shutting down. Shift your perspective by focusing on just one small step and thinking, *I can do this!*
- ❖ The Mindset *This isn't fair*, results in resistance, blame, and anger. Shift your perspective to *I am up for the challenge.*
- ❖ The Mindset *I have to do this my way* results in controlling and perfectionist traits. Shift your perspective to *I will do my best in the time I have.*

Here are a few more shifts:

- ❖ *I don't know where to start.* → *I'll pick a task and start there.*
- ❖ *I don't have time* or *It's not the right time.* → *There's no time like right now; I'll make the time.*
- ❖ *I can't do it all, so I shouldn't bother starting.* → *Every step, even a little one, makes a difference.*
- ❖ *I don't know how to . . .* → *I will get help or figure it out.*
- ❖ *I'm afraid of . . .* → *I will challenge my fearful thoughts and find a way to do it.*

Let me offer three ways to find a different perspective or Mindset:

1. What would someone else do? Think of a person who manages a certain type of situation well. Imagine what advice they'd offer you right now. What would they tell themselves to figure things out?
2. What is the opposite of what you're telling yourself? For example, *I can't do it* becomes *I can do it*.
3. Look outside and see what captures your eye, then jot it down on paper. For example, *The wind is blowing, the leaves are turning, and the air is clear*. Have fun with it! Find a perspective that works for you. Test it against your issue and see if it helps you shine a new light on your issue—pun intended.

   ❖ What do you notice in your surroundings? Name that.
   ❖ How does that make you feel?
   ❖ Turn that into a perspective.

Here are some examples:

❖ *The fog reminds me that my vision is blocked. If I cleared the fog, I could see everything better. My new perspective is clearing the fog. The fog represents my cloudy thoughts, the things I don't know, or perhaps an assumption I've made that needs more clarity.*
❖ *It's sunny outside. If I look at my issue from a sunny perspective, I'll shed light on it. I'll look for new information or clarity on things that feel like they're in the shadows. I'll identify what's working and do more of that.*

Examples of Shifting Mindsets

1. Issue: You're not sure how you'll accomplish something and are feeling stuck and blocked.

    ❖ Suggested Mindset: I'm curious about what is stopping me. I'm going to find and clear the block.

    ➢ Talk it through until you boil it down to your main limiting thought. That's the core roadblock that is keeping you stuck.
    ➢ Demystify the roadblock. Is it a limiting belief that isn't real? Can you debunk it and reframe your thoughts into something helpful?
    ➢ Explore new options with an open mind and accept that you'll be able to find your answer.

2. Issue: You're feeling overwhelmed because you don't know where to start on a project.

    ❖ Suggested Mindset: *I will take one step at a time.*

    ➢ Brainstorm possible steps to take.
    ➢ Start writing things down, and you'll realize you know more than you think.
    ➢ Select one step and plan when you'll begin.

3. Issue: You're afraid of making a big decision and committing to the outcome.

    ❖ Suggested Mindset: *I will use my values to decide between these options.*

    ➢ Ask yourself, Which option aligns with my values?

- Looking back a year from now, which decision would I be proud of?
- Who might I talk to with similar values to process my thoughts?

4. Issue: You're aware that you're putting off conversations for fear of stirring up conflict.

   ❖ Suggested Mindset: *I will build relationships through honesty, and I will seek to understand.*

   - Let go of being defensive—a very common relationship toxin.
   - Find your kindest voice and ask for their point of view.
   - Reflect on what they say.
   - Share your fears and point of view, from an authentic, vulnerable, and kind place.
   - Remember that it's okay to disagree with someone and not know how a conversation will turn out in the end.

> *Seek first to understand, then to be understood.*
> —Stephen Covey

Mindset Shift Stories

❖ Client's Struggle: A client gets stuck when trying to brainstorm ideas for her marketing and social media, a common problem for most entrepreneurs. Her brain shuts down after just a few ideas, and the Judge's voice shows up: Nothing you can write will be helpful. She gets anxious, stressed out, and feels terrible about herself.

➤ Results: She had a very short list of ideas and an even stronger negative self-image, leading to a lack of Action and an inconsistent marketing platform. She often moved on to something else or wasted several more hours ineffectively.

➤ Shift: When she noticed she was feeling stuck or judging herself, she would stop, breathe, and say something motivational such as *You can do this* or *No idea is a bad idea*.

➤ Tip: Be open to what might be helpful. For example, *I'll make a long list to brainstorm without editing as I go. Later, I'll go through it to pick the ideas I want to start with. I'll only eliminate ideas when I'm feeling calm and self-confident, not when my Saboteurs are having a heyday!*

➤ New Results: My client has been creating more marketing content while becoming more comfortable brainstorming. She has more Awareness of when her Judge shows up, but she no longer panics. She calms herself and looks for inspiration from her books and magazines, as well as from the client result list that she keeps at her desk. She has recruited a few friends to brainstorm with her, and she keeps a marketing journal labeled "Ideas to write about." Any time an idea pops into her head, she jots it down and refers back to it when it's time to write.

❖ Writer's Situation: My friend Kayleigh has a hobby of writing novels during National Novel Writing Month (November), with a goal of writing a complete novel in that time. One year, shortly after having her first child, she was struggling to find the time to write and shared her dilemma with some fellow writers. Kayleigh usually had well over twenty thousand words by mid-November, but this particular year she had only half that.

- ➢ Thankfully, she had a winning Mindset. She shared, "I am not giving up! I will write when I can and see what happens." This really fired up the group as she modeled persistence. *I am not giving up* can be a rallying cry for any situation. That kind of determination can be contagious. She also modeled self-care when she chose to accept that her writing would be different that year. Her unspoken Mindset was, *It's okay if I don't write as much. I'm spending quality time with my new baby.*

- ❖ Common Situation: You get behind and aren't meeting your goals.

  - ➢ Reaction: You feel defeated and judge yourself for "failing," even if you accomplished many tasks and had many obstacles in the way.
  - ➢ Alternate Response: Breathe. Tell yourself, *I have at least done something. I will keep at this.*
  - ➢ Results: You keep at it and do your best without beating yourself up.
  - ➢ Mindset Shift: *I'm pathetic* or *this is impossible* → *I've done more than I realized. Keep it up!*

At some point, you just have to take an issue and make a decision. Go this way or that. Do something or let it go. Say yes or say no. Using your Awareness, Acceptance, and Mindset, you can make the first decision. What will you do? Don't try to figure out how just yet. That comes next. Here are a few "Decision Statement" examples:

- ❖ I will put my house on the market.
- ❖ I will start looking for another job.
- ❖ I will offer a new product for my business.

- ❖ I will see the doctor about this nagging health issue.
- ❖ I will have a conversation to set better boundaries.

Exercise 38: Set a Decisive Mindset

1. Name your decisions, leaving out the words "try," "maybe," and "someday."

    I will _____

2. State the Mindset that will help you achieve your goal: _____.

STEP 4
ASSESSING

> *Until you believe you have options,
> you'll continue to feel stuck.*
> —Sean Stephenson, therapist, self-help author,
> and motivational speaker

Both the **Assessing** and Planning steps are part of the preparation phase of the Action Cycle. It's when you consider your options before you finalize your plan and take Action. Part of your assessment may have been deciding whether you'd address the issue yourself, delegate it to someone else, or dismiss it. I call this the **ADD Approach,** which involves three steps: address, delegate, and dismiss (see Table 8).

Table 8: *The ADD Approach*

Option	Thoughts for Each Option
Address	*I will do something about this.*
Delegate	*I will delegate this to someone else or perhaps hire someone.*
Dismiss	*I will not do this* or *I will do this at a later date.*

When you act without Assessing a situation first, you're acting from your habits, Survival Brain, and emotions. As the old saying goes, "The definition of insanity is doing the same thing over and over again and expecting different results." It takes an open mind to try something new and to get new results. If your mind is at ease and you're feeling like your Best Self, you're ready to make the best choices.

Do you remember finalizing your wedding reception location, selecting your college, or taking a new job? You probably didn't make any of those choices randomly; you looked at multiple options and then picked one. Making those decisions can be scary, but until you do you'll remain on the indecisive side of the equation. There's freedom and excitement on the other side!

At this point in the Action Cycle, you've decided to address an issue and have an empowered Mindset. You have a pretty good idea of what you want. Now you need to decide how to achieve it. Assess your options by brainstorming all the possibilities. Think outside of your usual box, and don't try to edit until you have a nice long list. I like to say, "Brainstorm without the edit button." Some of the best ideas come when our hearts and minds are open to possibilities. Get creative, playful, and collaborative. Consider actions that are the opposite of your norm. With the right Mindset, those possibilities can come flooding in, and it's up to you to capture them. To use a travel analogy, any travel app will give you a number of options for the mode of transportation and the route you can take. Getting from Point A to Point B isn't always a straight line. Sometimes you need to make detours, stop for gas, or stay in a hotel overnight. You may even need to take several modes of transportation.

My husband used to commute to his job in New York City by driving fifteen minutes to the train station, riding on the train for over an hour, taking a subway, and then walking the last ten minutes to his office in downtown Manhattan. If he looked only for a single mode of transportation from Point A to Point B, he might've been resigned to a very expensive taxi ride or a miserable car ride and high parking expenses.

Look at your options in the same way—there isn't just one answer. Do you break a project down into phases or a series of separate tasks? Do you collaborate with someone else for all or part of it? What will work best for you with your strengths and resources and bring you closest to your desired outcome? Later, you'll evaluate your list and make a decision, but for now, keep an open mind.

Brainstorming Tools

A typical "brainstorming" exercise is to make a list of every possible idea you have to meet your goal. You can get creative and use any number of tools to showcase your ideas, such as sticky notes, index cards, a whiteboard, or a large poster. Take your time and walk away if you're feeling stuck. When you come back to it, you might have a new perspective.

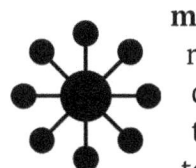

A great tool you can use to visualize all your options is a **mind map,** which is why I chose this symbol to represent Assessing. The objective is to write down as many ideas as you can without trying to edit or judge any answers. Start with your topic in a central bubble, along with your chosen Mindset. Each spoke off the central bubble is a possible option or category.

Here are some examples of topics and Mindsets.

- ❖ Finish writing my book with the *One hour at a time, one page at a time* Mindset.
- ❖ Get healthy with a *You can do this* Mindset.
- ❖ Set new boundaries around things or people who interrupt your workflow by adopting a *Focus on one thing at a time* Mindset.

Once you have your central theme with a goal and a Mindset, draw lines extending outward to each main category. Then each option can include related ideas or steps stemming from that main category. If it helps, you can start with a quick list or outline like mine below. Or you can skip right to drawing your own Get Healthy Mind Map.

- ❖ Goal: Get Healthy

  - ➢ Mindset: *Be proactive.*

    - ▪ Preventative Medicine

      - Annual physical
      - Preventative testing
      - Address health concerns (allergies, pains, digestive issues)

    - ▪ Self-care

      - Relaxing downtime
      - Exercise
      - Connections (friends, family, find group activities)

    - ▪ Healthy Eating

      - Mindful eating (read portion sizes, eat slowly, no eating after 8 p.m.)
      - Limit processed food (shop with a list, healthy snacking, less fast food)
      - More vegetables and water (plan meals, prep meals, keep water nearby)

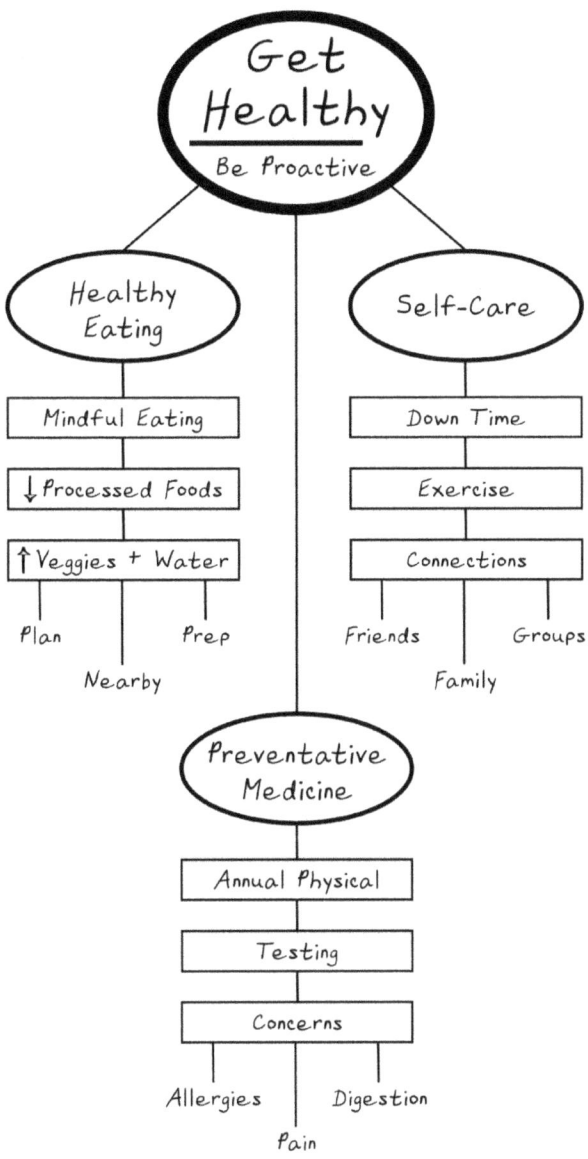

Get Healthy Mind Map: Central Bubble = Goal and Mindset; Second layer bubbles are possible categories of options; Next level is three main ideas for each category and additional options for one.

For this type of goal, you may choose to do many things, but probably not all at once. What options do you focus on first? Is anything mentioned in more than one category? Which options do you let go of or try later is up to you, and with everything laid out for you on paper, the decision is usually clearer. Still unsure? Pick one direction to start (think Easing In).

I find it extremely helpful to talk things through with someone, both for brainstorming and for developing my plan (as part of the next step). This conversation partner could be completely unrelated to the goal, or they could have a vested interest in it. An ideal brainstorming partner stays open-minded, offers options, and asks questions rather than advising or telling you what to do.

If there's anyone else involved in the issue, be sure to get their feedback or you'll cause another problem while missing the opportunity for more input. With the right boundaries, even a Controller can see the value of new ideas. Some people need time to process, so be mindful of others' needs. Ask them what would help them produce the best ideas.

Whatever issue you've decided to work on, be sure to start the Assessing step with a calm and grounded mood instead of when you are feeling triggered or anxious. Choose your decisive Mindset, and then start the brainstorming session. Let yourself go. No idea is a bad idea. Any idea could lead to a great idea! Tell your Judge, Perfectionist, Naysayer, or any other brake-pushing inner part to take a back seat while you sit in the driver's seat as your Best Self.

Assess your options with an open mind and make your final decision at a later time.

The Treetop Planner

While I was training to be a coach, I created a tool to help me keep track of the tasks I needed to do for school, my daughter's upcoming wedding, and assorted other tasks. I called the tool my **Treetop Planner**, as if I were looking down on my life from my childhood three-story tree in my backyard and each box was another "yard." Each box represented a category—a major project or an area of my life such as health, family, finances, or school. Depending on what's going on in my life, the categories I focus on change.

If you're trying to stay on top of key goals in many areas of your life, begin by writing out every category of your life in a separate box, and include a box for any upcoming major goal (like a wedding or a move). Then list all the upcoming tasks in each box. The idea is to jot down the list of tasks that might be swimming in your head so that they have a place where you can review and prioritize them. When you see everything in front of you, it's easier to decide what to do next.

I find it helpful to make one column just for my business. You might make a column for each member of your family. The column headings aren't necessary, but I included them in Table 9 along with an example for each category.

Table 9: *Sample Treetop Planner*

Business Tasks	Family/ Personal Tasks	Upkeep Tasks
Business Planning ❖ Next quarter themes	Family ❖ Pick a reunion date	Finances ❖ Monthly bills
Client Time & Communication ❖ Follow-up emails	Friends/Social ❖ Buy concert tickets	House ❖ Call plumber
Next Webinar: ❖ create, set date, marketing	Fun/Travel ❖ Packing list for trip	Medical/Health ❖ Shingles vaccine
Invoicing/Bills ❖ Invoice new client	Personal Project ❖ Finish stuffed animal for Lucia	Papers! ❖ Purge all mail and newspapers

If you want to make big sweeping changes in your life, it's helpful to take this holistic approach. Consider all aspects of your life, as they will likely all be affected. You might be looking for work-life harmony and will focus on all the key activities you'd like to do on a regular basis. What does work-life harmony look like to you? Which major categories would you include? What activities would make you happy? You might include fun time, exercise, healthy eating, reading, relaxation, and/or nature time.

Remember that anything you add to your daily or weekly list will probably require removing something else. What will you say yes to, and what will you say no to? A client of mine realized she never made time for her business Planning—it was never on her priority list. She kept telling herself, *I'll get around to it when I have time.* After discussing the topic for most of a coaching session, she realized she needed to schedule business-building tasks into her calendar just like she does with her client and networking meetings. The topic then became a higher priority, and with that Planning time, she was able to implement many of the ideas she had ignored for over a year.

> **Story: Expo**
>
> Lindsey has a service-based business and is a solo entrepreneur with no employees. Her business relies solely on her ability to attract clients and give them great service.
>
> She decided to sign up for a tabletop expo to increase interest in her business, grow her sales funnel, and perhaps gain some clients. The expo was geared toward her target market, so it was the perfect opportunity to connect with people. She had about a month to prepare and many decisions to make, which made her feel a little overwhelmed and indecisive. She was struggling to find just the right approach. Her thinking was, *The date is on my calendar, and I'm mentally committed to it. Now what?*
>
> Lindsey was feeling overwhelmed by the number of options. When it came to Assessing options in this circumstance, she found it helpful to talk through it with someone who had done it before— me. This is an example of using your resources

to help you, which makes it easier to accelerate your Action.

After brainstorming, Lindsey needed clarity in these three categories:

1. Something to attract people to come to her table

    a. Visual display items
    b. Giveaway items

2. Something to engage people and a way to learn more about her offer(s)

    a. A focus of interest based on her business
    b. An opening question she could ask people as they approached her table

3. A way to collect names of people who showed interest in her business

    a. A survey, game, or drawing; something they could fill out
    b. A piece of paper and pen to collect names and emails
    c. A prize drawing as an enticement

Lindsey and I discussed what she wanted the participants to know about her business, what could engage them, and how she could best translate that into a big display graphic for her table. In the past, she'd presented webinars about her business and had some exceptional graphics that visually explained the shift she helps her clients through. She also knew the kinds of questions a typical person would ask before they might hire her. These thought bubbles became part of her display.

After our conversation, Lindsay was able to make quick decisions and set about creating her display. She devised a survey for participants to share their thoughts on a particular subject, a way to sign up for her survey results, and boxes to check if they wanted a follow-up consultation. Once her display information was ready, she recruited her sister to practice with her so that she would feel prepared on the day of the expo.

Exercise 39: Assess

Ask yourself these questions: *What do I want, and do these options help me get there? Is there something else I haven't thought of yet?* You can also imagine yourself as someone who's already completed the task or solved the problem. Think about what they did and ask yourself, *Who did they have to be in order to take care of things?* Channel your inner wisdom, take on your Best Self Mindset, and brainstorm! Everything is possible. Once you have a good list of options, you can begin to see how some will fit your plan better than others.

> After the Assessing step of the Action Cycle, your abbreviated notes should include these items:
>
> 1. My issue is _____.
> 2. The biggest thing I am aware of is _____.
> 3. My biggest potential obstacle might be _____.
> 4. I accept _____.
> 5. What I want is _____.
> 6. My empowering Mindset is _____.
> 7. My options are _____, _____, _____.

Whittle Down Your Choices

After you have a good list of options, select the steps that will become part of your plan. This is the point where many people get stuck. They know what they *could* do, but now they have to act on what they *will* do. It's another shift to make. There's something scary or final about putting these steps into your plan because the commitment level has gotten higher.

Remember your empowered Mindset and your why. Instead of listening to Fear or Procrastination, let your Best Self come forward to be in charge of selecting and Planning. Don't try to do this work when you're upset or frustrated. Listen with your head, your heart, and your gut as you evaluate your options, knowing that if you try something new, you can adjust your plan later if it doesn't work out.

There are two typical approaches to selecting from a list of options: evaluate each option separately, or look at all the options together to compare and contrast until the best idea bubbles to the surface. You may also find that your ultimate plan includes several options, as in my Get Healthy Mind Map. You may also want to consider what else is going on in your life and how these options might impact other projects or priorities.

Generally, you'll go through the pros and cons of your options or evaluate the potential outcome of each. For business decisions, you might look at the **return on investment** or the **expected value** or benefit of each decision—you're evaluating what you'll gain in either money, results, or anything else of value from an investment you make of your time, money, or energy. Will you make a profit? Will you have a beneficial outcome? When you're dealing with a very personal or emotional decision, however, it's never that clear-cut; there are a lot more variables to consider and much more at stake. If the goal involves habits you want to develop or ways to make you feel happier, it can be even more challenging to use logic or reasoning. Listen to your gut, and trust that you know yourself best.

Monitor your thoughts. If you slip back into listening to your Perfectionist who believes that *there's only one right way to do things*, you could end up in analysis paralysis. Rather than trying to find a needle in a haystack, why not start somewhere? Ask yourself, *Of all the things on this list, what's the one thing I could do right now?*

STEP 5
PLANNING

If you fail to plan, you plan to fail.

—proverbial wisdom, anonymous origin

A plan is a well-defined description of all the steps you intend to take to achieve your desired outcome.

Bigger outcomes require more SMART goals and more detailed **Planning**. Listing the who, what, where, and when of the full project (and steps as needed) helps keep you on course and prepared for each new phase of the project.

No issue or project lives in a vacuum. There's always something else going on that will distract or detract from our actions. This is one of the many reasons to start Planning before taking Action. Here are some other reasons:

1. Planning helps you stay focused. You know what the next step is, and your restless mind doesn't have a chance to lure you off track. You can anticipate obstacles that might affect your outcomes, such as time, money, other people, the weather, competing goals, and other potential difficulties, then make those hypotheticals part of your plan.

    ❖ Where will you hold the ceremony if it rains?
    ❖ How will you get two projects done in the same time frame?
    ❖ What will help you manage your time when hosting an event for twenty-five people?

    ➢ What can you do ahead of time?
    ➢ Who will help do what?

    - Write out a timeline for the day.
    - Walk through it mentally the day before.
    - Plan to get enough sleep!

2. Planning gives you breathing room to see the big picture and how the steps work together. By Planning, you may identify an issue or solve how to manage manpower, resources, downtime, and priorities.
3. Planning allows you to recruit help and effectively assign tasks. Businesses, restaurants, manufacturers, and institutions rely on Planning as a key focal point for execution. They have their business plan, marketing plan, and project plans all funneling into their monthly and daily activity plans.

In my experience, most people don't do enough Planning to maximize their desired results for their health, home, family, and job. I might sound like a very organized, task-focused person, but actually my true inclination is to be a Free Spirit with few routines and plenty of flexibility. That's why Planning has become so important for me—it doesn't come naturally. But anyone can improve their habits if they work at it. Many of us live with the chaos of competing goals and too many to-dos, and our parts don't see the big picture of how they all could work together in harmony. Instead, they fight with each other. Planning gives us the opportunity to prioritize and make the situation work rather than struggle haphazardly.

Smaller tasks or projects don't necessarily require a five-page project plan, but they can always use some basic Planning; for example, "At 9 a.m. tomorrow, I will start Task A" (the one you're dreading most). Ideally, that plan includes the task, how long it might take, and where you will do it. The more specific your plan is, the more likely you'll get it done. Perhaps most importantly, you'll also plan what to tell yourself to be sure you don't let any other issue (or inner part) get in your way or supersede your Action.

You can also incorporate habit stacking into your plan. For instance, you could add a time block to follow after you brush your teeth each morning that includes time for meditating, journaling, Planning your day, or any other task you deem important.

Add Structure, Creativity, and Fun

> **Setting goals is just one step toward success. Establishing habits and systems to support those goals is the key to long-term results and growth.**

One way to fortify your plan for success is to add structure—perhaps a routine, system, or checklist—and incorporate strategies and opportunities for being creative and having fun. You can create ways to stay engaged with your goal, which will increase your likelihood of succeeding. There are many ways to set up structure and support for your goals. Have fun with it! Here are some examples:

- ❖ **Accountability.** Tell your friends so they know what you're working on, and/or find a buddy to join you in your goal.
- ❖ **Process your thoughts.** Talk your plan through with someone.
- ❖ **Create a routine.** Put small steps together in a certain order that's easy to repeat.

- ❖ **Use an app.** There are any number of apps you can use to track your goals. You can even use them to gain support and accountability.
- ❖ **Schedule.** Make time for your goal and for fun. It won't magically happen; there will always be other things to do. Put specific time blocks on your calendar.
- ❖ **Add breaks and music.** A Mindset of *all work and no play* decreases your will to keep going.
- ❖ **See it, do it.** Use visual cues to motivate you. Look at the tasks and habits that would support your goal, then create a chart or a vision board. Make it bright, colorful, and fun. Leave it out in the open so you can check things off and easily see your progress.
- ❖ **Add a track-and-reward system.** Add to your visual cues the phrase, "When I reach each step I get to," then fill in the rewards you'll celebrate with. Using colorful charts and adding goals such as saving money for clothes or taking a trip if you earn enough points are ideas my clients and I have used over the years. Tip: stay away from food rewards.

Plan for Obstacles

One of the best ways to reach success for any goal is Planning for obstacles, distractions, and outside interferences. Identify your biggest potential obstacle, such as being easily distracted, and create a plan to outsmart it. This will help you not only proactively get past obstacles but make doing so fun and creative.

If you're distracted by your smartphone or electronic notifications, there are ways to overcome this. You can delete games that waste your time and can set the do-not-disturb feature during work hours so that you aren't distracted by notifications. If your phone is really a problem, put it in a hard-to-reach location so that you're mindful every time you pick it up or glance at it.

One more option is an exercise I learned in my coach training that allows you to list all the ways you can make your plan more successful—what you will say yes to and no to. Think of them as guidelines and boundaries. It's simple enough to say, "I will do X." It's another thing to carry it out, especially if you have constant interruptions or demands of your time, such as meetings that pop into your calendar all day or personal demands as a parent or caregiver. Are you regretting joining the board of your condo? Have you overcommitted to things that no longer seem important but you're still doing them? Do you get distracted by your environment? What can you do about it?

The biggest tip is to prioritize your goal and add the **Yes/No Exercise** to the Planning step of the Action Cycle. For instance, if you want to stay on task during work hours but have thought of other things you want to take care of, you can say no to task-switching and say yes to keeping a list of things to get back to later. Set aside an hour at some point in the day to focus on whatever needs addressing.

Exercise 40: Prepare Your Yes/No List

1. Name your goal.
2. Fill in the YES column with rules, guidelines, steps, or boundaries you will say yes to in order to take Action and achieve your goal.
3. Fill in the NO column with the types of things that interrupt your workflow and life balance or any other distractions you want to say no to.

What Will I Say YES to in Order to Succeed?	What Will I Say NO to in Order to Succeed?

Game Your Plan

To game your plan is to find ways of making any plan more fun and creative while also being proactive about typical obstacles. It's a strategy I created for myself to increase the likelihood that I could meet one of my goals. If you know which tendencies are likely to hijack your progress, such as avoidance or struggling with time management, then gaming your plan is a way to beat them.

> I typically set a goal to walk more frequently prior to going on vacation so that I have the endurance I'll need for a busy trip. In 2010, before Steve and I went on a tour of Rome and a Mediterranean cruise, I set a goal to walk sixty miles—the approximate circumference of Rome. I created a chart to log my distance as I walked each day and kept it on my refrigerator with colored pencils to fill it in.
>
> If I had set my goal to only "walk frequently," I might've accomplished that task. Yet when I gamed my plan—giving it a theme, adding a colorful chart, and making it more fun—I increased my chances of achieving my goal. When I didn't

feel like taking a walk, all I had to do was look at my chart and I was inspired to walk, even if it was only half a mile. The Adventurer part of me enjoyed imagining where I was walking, and the Calculating part of me got to track my progress on a colorful chart. My Optimist said, *Every little bit counts.*

I specifically remember looking at my chart about a week before we were leaving and seeing that I had to pick up my pace to reach my goal. I put on my sneakers and took a three-mile walk that day, bringing me closer to my finish line. By the time I'd spent a few days in Rome, I was grateful to be in such good shape. It's hard to have fun when you're tired and your legs hurt.

Fast forward to the spring of 2021, a year into the pandemic, and I was barely getting any exercise. My right hip was bothering me, so I started walking a few times a week, Planning to build up my strength and test whether my hip was an urgent issue or just a little challenge to be dealt with. In May and June, I tracked my walking trips—a total of thirty-eight miles. I felt like I was making progress, and my hip was getting stronger and felt less painful. In August, I went on vacation to the Poconos with my daughters and their families. I was extremely grateful to have started walking again. My new Fitbit tracked thirty miles in one week, and I was able to enjoy myself while I kept up with the kids and grandkids.

When we booked a trip to Ireland, I decided to set a goal of walking the distance of our week-long bus tour: from Dublin to Kilkenny, then to Cork, the Cliffs of Moher, Ashford Castle, and back to Dublin. Though my original goal was six hundred miles by June 30, 2022, I actually walked a total of 985 miles in a year. I tracked my progress on a newly purchased map of Ireland, putting markers up as I reached key cities. By the time we left for Ireland, I had walked almost the entire circumference of the island before ever getting on the plane. My hip never hurt no matter how much we walked on the tour.

We can use creativity and fun with our system of inner parts too. I believe everyone has inner parts that battle over taking Action—one for and the other against. We have a natural tendency at different times in our lives to have one foot on the gas and another on the brake. We can devise a way to make the most of our helpful parts and isolate or cancel out our distracting parts.

If you're writing a book, for example, you don't want your Doubtful part to show up more often than your Expressive part. What inspires and amplifies your Action part while quieting your Hesitant part is different from person to person. To help my writing, I created a mind map with all the topics I wanted to cover in the book. At any given time, if I felt stuck I could pick a topic and have something to write about. I later had to deal with how it all fit together, but for those moments when I was staring at a blank page, I had a plan to help me put words on paper.

When you want to work on a project or tackle a thorny issue, you want your Best Self to be in charge, not your Avoider. Think about what inspires you and remember your why. Allow yourself to get excited, and acknowledge the Doubtful and Afraid parts of you. Incorporate ways to assuage your Doubtful part. What adds gas to your tank so that you can take Action?

Exercise 41: Pump the Gas or Push the Brakes

Explore and get familiar with your inner parts, then game your plan to stifle the Brake-Pushers while energizing the Action-Takers.

1. What parts of you push the brake?
2. What parts of you step on the gas?
3. How will you game your plan to accelerate your goal or make it more enjoyable?

Create a Clear Plan

Depending on the specifics of your project or issue, your plan can be really simple or quite elaborate, possibly with phases and a long timeline. Having a plan makes it much easier to take laser-focused Action and achieve your goal. As you develop your plan, you're creating a roadmap of how you'll get this project done. Now it's time to create a clear plan for your goal.

Consider these tips as you go through the who, what, when, where, and why questions of Planning:

- ❖ **Phase**: If the project is really big, put the steps into phases and give each phase a time frame. As the steps in Phase 1 are gaining momentum, look into Phase 2 and see what you need to start doing.
- ❖ **Prioritize**: Look at the biggest steps and determine the best order to do them in. However, be willing to modify the plan if you learn something new or the plan changes.

- **Schedule**: As opposed to assuming that you'll find the time to get them done, block off time on your schedule for specific tasks. At the end of one day or phase, look ahead to see what's next.
- **Identify**: Are other people involved in this project? They could be partners, collaborators, supporters, or detractors. Do you need to set boundaries with, delegate to, or gain support from anyone?
- **Incorporate:** Use visuals, charts, or whiteboards to stay on track. Incorporate creative ways to track and celebrate your progress.
- **Anticipate:** Plan how to resume if you get off track. Incorporate a list of potential obstacles by gaming your plan and filling in a Yes/No chart. Don't forget this step!

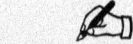

Exercise 42: Plan

Now it's time to write out your plan, incorporating your responses to the following prompts:

1. Name your goal.
2. Name your empowered, decisive Mindset.
3. Write your outcome statement: "I am the person who did [X] because [Y]." (You may prefer to start with "I want to" or "I will.")
4. Establish your start date and desired completion date.
5. If it's a big project, identify what phases you might include (each with its own desired completion date). Give each phase a name.

6. Name the Action steps you'll take (possibly SMART goals).
7. Name the strategies that will help you succeed, such as time blocking, prioritizing, delegating, and making a Yes/No list.
8. Create ways to track your progress with built-in steps to celebrate and ways to reward yourself (or your team).
9. Answer the question, "What type(s) of maintenance will this outcome require once completed?" If you need to, finalize your goal maintenance plan after the Reflection step.
10. Decide whether to share this plan with someone else. If more than one person is involved in the project, I suggest creating the plan together. You can create your own individualized plan for your part in the project.

STEP 6
ACTION

> *A moment of clarity without any action is just a thought that passes in the wind. But a moment of clarity followed by an action is a pivotal moment in our life.*
>
> —Don Miguel Ruiz Jr.

You've taken the time to dig into your issue, gain clarity, and create a plan of **Action**, hopefully helping you to feel decisive and motivated. You know what you want and have determined the best options for how to achieve it. Your plan may include basic steps or be more intricate with phases, steps, and a detailed timeline. Now it's time to use that plan to take Action. Every move you make, day in and day out, is an Action that either serves you or doesn't.

Action begets more Action.

Action Steps

There are different kinds of Action steps. Some are larger while others are smaller baby steps toward your goal. Making a phone call, organizing a shelf, hiring a new employee, and taking a break every ninety minutes are all Action steps. So are scheduling, Planning, and spending quality time with loved ones. Larger desired outcomes, such as selecting a college, decluttering the house, or running a conference, will need to be broken down into more manageable steps. Some steps, large or small, may take longer to complete than others. Don't forget to allow a bit of breathing room in your timeline for Reflection once you've taken Action. Rushing from one Action to another probably won't save you any time, and you may add undue stress or miss something important.

Looking at your list so far, did you break down any larger goals into smaller tasks? If this is a long-term goal, what phases have you planned and in what order? When I became a coach, I went through several phases and steps. Phase 1, becoming a coach, involved selecting a coaching school, arranging for travel, taking the courses, and finding sample clients. Phase 2 was every entrepreneur's big hurdle—launching my business. I had to create a website, define my niche of ideal clients (which has changed many times over fifteen years), create an intake process, decide on pricing, and start networking while asking for referrals.

While that was going on, Phase 3 began, which was getting my certification. I really wanted the legitimacy that having a credential would give me, especially since I was changing careers so drastically. I took an advanced, twenty-five-week course, coached more than five clients for six months, and eventually took a written and oral exam. I also resigned from my job as a respiratory therapist and joined the International Coaching Federation.

Ultimately, it took me over eighteen months to complete all three phases. Some people might've chosen to take a break or skip Phase 3, but I was determined to complete the full training because it was important to me. Since that time, launching my business has morphed into a whole new goal of growing my business.

One of the best things I did that supported my journey was pairing up with one of my classmates, Anna Cole, who was my partner in developing the Awareness to Action process. We became each other's clients, friends, and biggest cheerleaders. We brainstormed our Action steps together and coached each other into taking actions we may never have taken otherwise. I'll always be grateful to Anna for her friendship and partnership.

Make a List and Do It!

My husband and I live in a historic old home on one and a half acres with many gardens, a small pond, mature trees, and a large, detached garage. We really love the property, but it requires a lot of upkeep. I love to feed the fish in the pond, and I'll take an occasional turn at weeding, but even when wearing gloves I invariably end up with a rash. It turns out I'm allergic to most things in the garden, especially the weeds.

    One summer, we were less than a week away from hosting an outdoor birthday party. Due to COVID-19, it had been several years since we'd hosted our large family, and I wanted everything to look its best. Unfortunately, there were many glaring tasks to take care of around the yard, and we'd been busy the prior weekends. It was Memorial Day, and I knew Steve wanted to spend the day enjoying some much-earned downtime, so I felt a little guilty even bringing up the task list. He worked very long days, and I had my allergy limitations. I remembered reading once that if you really care about something, you should be willing to put in the effort to take care of it. I wanted our property to look great, and I knew we were quickly running out of time to get it all done. So I brought up the yard work and offered to help.

    Taking a "tour of the estate," our nickname for walking around the yard, Steve and I made an extensive list of all the tasks that needed our attention, twenty-five items total. We agreed that we'd tackle only what was urgent or what we'd be able to finish within four hours, leaving time for a relaxing dinner. We each took assignments and got busy. I pruned boxwoods and hydrangeas, moved stacks of firewood, pulled some weeds, and loaded the pickup truck with all the debris. Steve cut small saplings along the driveway, buzzed weeds, and whacked tall grass along the stone walls and foundation. He also pulled creeping myrtle from the rhododendrons and tall weeds out of our patio garden.

In all, we crossed fourteen items off the list in our allotted time. Not bad! We made a decision, focused our attention, prioritized, and stayed motivated. It was 100 percent a team effort for a short period of time that made a huge difference. We zipped through most of the Action Cycle: Awareness, Acceptance, Mindset, Assessing, Planning, and Action. As for our Reflection, we realized that our Planning helped keep us focused. Working together made it feel less like work and more like a collaboration. Our to-do list will never be complete because there's always something else to do, but we made a really big dent in it. We even chose items that would normally be put off for the future. In the end, we felt very proud of our effort.

I never want to take Steve's hard work for granted. I am deeply aware of the amount of work it takes to keep our yard and gardens looking beautiful. I'd love to say that I'll help more often. However, I recently ended up at the doctor's office again—this time for swollen bug bites and a rash. Sadly, I think my big-effort days will have to find a new project indoors!

The big takeaway for collaborative projects is to embrace the challenge, collaborate, assign tasks, and use the Action Cycle.

Enjoy the Journey

Goals! Sometimes you get tired of thinking about them. If it feels like too much pressure and your commitment is waning, then it's time to try something new. It's time to add ways to enjoy the journey and game your plan. Try a few of the following strategies:

- ❖ Strategy: Celebrate Your Wins.

    It's important to your well-being to take your foot off the gas from time to time and see what you've accomplished. What are you seeing and feeling?

- ❖ Strategy: Build Momentum

    What is your favorite part of the outcome you're working toward? Is there something you just can't wait to experience? Perhaps there's a way to get a taste of it now—a way to feel the excitement and pride with one small step. Here are a few examples:

    - ➢ Organize one little space and take a picture to share with someone.
    - ➢ Prepare your favorite healthy meal and invite a friend to join you.

- ➢ Write something funny that doesn't have to be posted, edited, or tweaked to perfection.
- ➢ Pick up the phone and call someone you want to connect with.

- ❖ Strategy: Take a Break

    Maybe you'd benefit from a day of doing nothing. Perhaps you just need to breathe, read a book, or take a slow, quiet walk in the woods. We all need to take some time to smell the roses—to focus on our own self-care and notice what's going on around us without all the rush and intentions and lists of things to do. What makes your journey a little more joyful? Partnering with a friend? Taking short breaks? Celebrating small wins?

- ❖ Strategy: Add Self-Care

    A recent story of enjoying self-care and being consistently committed came with a twenty-first-century twist. I started doing yoga three times a week with my daughter Melissa. She's very good at following consistent routines, so I thought if I asked her to buddy up with me I'd stick with it. The twist is that Melissa lives six hours away and we do everything through video chat.

    This was my first attempt at exercising three times a week. The Free Spirit in me resists structure. It's a bit of a luxury taking a full hour for our routine, but it has become a great way for us to burn a few calories and help this aging grammie build strength, flexibility, and balance. I've learned the sunrise salutation as well as many standing poses.

    The first time I tried standing poses I could keep my balance for only about ten seconds. I looked out the window for something to focus on and saw a woodpecker nibbling away at the suet feeder. It was a ladder-backed woodpecker about eight inches long with a red head. My daughter Melissa is a redhead too.

Today, I think about the woodpecker every time I get ready for yoga. It gives me something fun to watch for, and it keeps me present and connected to my surroundings instead of thinking about other things I could be doing instead of yoga. According to several websites, the woodpecker is a spirit animal that represents intuition, opportunity, communication, listening, innovation, and determination. Noticing that woodpecker was my intuition—that inner part— telling me that I was taking this opportunity to test my determination. Now I enjoy communicating with my daughter as I listen to the voice inside me saying, *This is good for you*!

One day, I was going to finish yoga a little early to build in a break before another appointment. I was starting to feel a little wimpy for quitting, and then I saw the woodpecker. I decided to stick with the session for a little bit longer until the bird left. I guess the bird has now become my accountability partner too!

The whole point of this story is that I have a lifelong goal—to increase my balance and strength through exercise and to live a healthier, happier life—and found a way to make pursuing that goal fun. I include my daughter and occasional conversations with my grandkids, I have an accountability partner who keeps showing up, and now I have my woodpecker to watch for. The good news is that I can now hold my balance poses for forty seconds, and my flexibility and strength are improving. My husband has even joined in since his recent retirement. *Ease and flow. Enjoy the journey.*

Exercise 43: Enjoy the Journey

Now it's your turn to find ways to enjoy the journey so that you'll stay on the Action path to Completion.

1. What does the phrase "enjoy the journey" mean to you?
2. What would you like to enjoy doing more often?
3. If you took one little chunk of a goal and found a way to celebrate, what would you choose to do?
4. What version of gaming your plan might help you enjoy the journey and stay in Action?
5. If you could pick a spirit animal to inspire you from time to time, what animal might it be, and what would its message be telling you?

General Strategies for the Action Step

1. **Design your environment**. Action steps that seem scary or new require more of our energy, belief, commitment, and confidence than simple tasks. According to my friend and fellow coach Vinny Liscio, they may also require a little environmental design to allow for success rather than failure. Does your home, office, and/or support system help you reach your goals? How might you design things a little differently to improve your success rate? Are there any boundaries you need to set with those around you?

2. **Create routines**. If you look at the steps in your Action plan, you'll probably see categories of actions. There may be things you'll do daily and steps you'll have to do only once. This is a good time to apply habit stacking. What actions can be grouped into a process, habit, or routine that you do frequently? Morning routines, bedtime routines, and meal routines are particularly good places to insert health-related steps such as meditation, exercise, or drinking more water.

3. **Minimize task switching**. Evaluate how often you switch tasks. Work routines that include answering emails, making phone calls, collecting data, or going to meetings can make or break your day. Hopefully, your plan includes ways to minimize the time loss and maximize the efficiency of these routines. This is especially important for those with **high switching costs**, meaning they have trouble staying focused and productive while switching between tasks.

4. **Embrace task-stacking**. When you group similar tasks together, you work more efficiently. For example, you can make a group of phone calls or write a series of emails rather than switching back and forth between the two. Also, focus on one task at a time in order to make headway. If you work from home, don't try to juggle work with laundry and grocery shopping just because (you think) you can.

5. **Develop personalized strategies**. Create strategies that will make a difference in your results. They might include setting boundaries around time, laying out clear communication, or saying no for the first time. Whatever they are, implement new strategies as you go, especially if you find that you're struggling in a particular area. Some may be scary

or out of your comfort zone, but they might also be game-changing. You'll have exactly what you need to refocus and get back on track.

Tips to Overcome Feeling Stuck

- ❖ Refer to your plan regularly, keeping it front and center.
- ❖ Have an accountability buddy to keep you honest.
- ❖ Remember your why.
- ❖ Visualize the future with this issue resolved or the project completed.
- ❖ Celebrate your wins as you accomplish baby steps.
- ❖ Notice any resistance, name it, and ask yourself why it's present.
- ❖ Name the emotions present, then explore and challenge them.
  - ➢ If you feel fearful, what are you afraid of and how can you reframe your thinking?
  - ➢ If you feel outside of your comfort zone, what's one small stretch you could try?
  - ➢ If you feel overwhelmed, pick a starting point until you get back into the groove.
- ❖ Decisiveness, excitement, and hope—uplifting emotions—might be present, but you may find them beneath louder negative emotions coming from other parts.
  - ➢ Explore what sabotaging parts are present.
  - ➢ Ask them to step back so your Best Self can be in charge.

- Name your Mindset. Is it problem-focused? Shift to your empowered Mindset.
- Which finest and best skills and characteristics do you want to call on to take Action?
- Breathe, calm your system down, and let your Best Self take the lead.
- Assess the actions you're taking and how frequently. What is one more step that will show you're committed to your goal?
- Explore any possible competing goals. Do you have to decide which to focus on, or can it be both? If you can't focus on them at the same time, perhaps your Mindset can be *If this, then that.*
- You may think, *I don't have time.*
  - Ask yourself if this is really true.
  - What are you making time for?
  - Is there a little shift that might allow time for your goal?
  - Are you picking the easy tasks and leaving your highest priority goal for the morsels of time you find? How can you flip that?
- There's more than just being too busy. Are other things taking priority, and is that okay?
- Reframe any limiting beliefs such as these:
  - *I have to get it all done at once.*
  - *If I don't get it done by X, it won't be worth it.*
  - *I'm not meant to be doing this; I don't have the _____ to achieve it.*

- ❖ Is this the right time for this goal? Only you can answer this truthfully. Take some time to ponder your answer. If you come back with a *yes*, then it's time to put your goal front and center in your mind and in your life.

Execution Tips

- ❖ Do the harder steps first, whenever you can. You're fresher at the top of the day, especially if you do a little mindfulness breathing or meditation.
- ❖ Give yourself credit for every step you take. Focus on the ten things you did rather than beating yourself up for the one thing you didn't do.
- ❖ When you plan to work on something for hours at a time, be sure to build in breaks and use a timer to remind yourself it's time to get back to it.
- ❖ If you're really dreading a task, start with a short period of time at first and build up from there. Be sure to pat yourself on the back for anything you accomplish.
- ❖ Set up a plan for each day, week, or month's work.

    - ➢ Each evening, plan what to accomplish the next day, including the first thing you'll do.
    - ➢ Plan your week on Sunday night or Monday morning.
    - ➢ At the end of each month, plan what you intend to accomplish the following month.

Exercise 44: Become Aware of Your Actions

If you find yourself feeling stuck, or rationalizing about not taking enough action, ask yourself the following questions. The answers should guide you toward new Awareness and perhaps a new plan of action.

1. What is going well? (You might be doing better than you thought.)
2. Am I my Best Self right now? If I feel triggered or anxious, what can I do to calm down, release the worry, and restart with an empowered Mindset?
3. What am I committed to? What am I saying yes to and what am I saying no to?
4. Is there someone else working on the same goal at this time who I could partner with?
5. If this is a long-term goal, are there ways to break it into phases? Could I start with Phase 1 now as a way of Easing In?
6. Am I hesitating because I feel like this isn't the right time?

    → Is there anything I should complete first before I take on this task?
    → Is now better than later? Why or why not?
    → If I don't do it now, will I lose an opportunity? Will my choices disappear? Is that okay?

7. Am I heading into some major life change that will make this goal difficult to pursue (such as surgery, moving, having a child, getting ready to retire, or taking care of an ill family member)? In other words, is there a good reason for the hesitation or delay? If I delay, when might I do this, and are there smaller tasks I can get started on now? (Note: This doesn't mean you can't pursue the goal, but it helps to have realistic expectations.)
8. What will I commit to do today?

STEP 7
COMPLETION

> *Success is completion. Success is being able to complete what we set out to do—each individual action, each specific step, each desired experience whether a big project or a very small errand.*
>
> —Susan Ford Collins, *Our Children Are Watching*

As I approached the concept of Action during my own journey, I leaned on the idea that if I was stuck in a doubtful Mindset and not taking action, I could use certain tools and frameworks to help me become decisive and move into Action, similar to clearing up a traffic jam. What I eventually realized is that decisiveness doesn't always lead to Action and **Completion**. Saying I will do something doesn't make it happen.

Sometimes we need more than a decisive mind to complete what we started.

Though we make a number of decisions, we don't act on all of them, and even fewer make it all the way to Completion. Sometimes we go from doubtful to decisive to Action and then get stuck or give up. Take any New Year's Resolution as an example. Your heart and mind decided on something, you started acting on the goal, and then reality hit. You lost your confidence or commitment. Something happened that created a distraction or a new hurdle to overcome. You believed you could do it, and then doubts crept in. You weren't sure what to do or how to do it, nor how to keep it up. Maybe you decided it was too hard, then your Rationalizer chimed in thinking, *Maybe it wasn't the right goal after all*. Poof! Your New Year's Resolution is last week's news.

Here are some possible challenges to be aware of during the transition from Action to Completion:

- ❖ Fear
- ❖ A loss of interest or waning enthusiasm
- ❖ A lack of time
- ❖ Losing sight of the desired outcome or end zone
- ❖ Competing goals
- ❖ Distractions
- ❖ Lack of prioritization and time management
- ❖ Setbacks that lower your confidence
- ❖ Mental fortitude

What helps you overcome those obstacles and propels you all the way to Completion? We already know that commitment, belief, and confidence are crucial, but we need to add three more qualities: clarity, perseverance, and courage.

Clarity is knowing what you need to know to move forward. You need a clear goal, a clear reason the goal is important, clarity around the steps you will take, and a plan to achieve it: *I know what to do and when.* Perseverance, like confidence, is a trait that gets stronger over time and with experience: *I won't give up!* Courage is **s**ometimes needed to overcome our fears and set boundaries with others. Courage to start in the first place, and then courage to stay strong when the going gets tough. It comes from within and is often bolstered by having a support system to hold you up and give you fortitude. Small successes and baby steps can build courage: *It might be scary, but I'll try.*

Completion Strategies

Beyond these three qualities, there are other strategies available to you at any time:

- Remember your why—why is this important to you, and why now. Revisit your why as often as possible and any time you feel like you are struggling.
- Explore the big picture of your project and what life will be like after it is done. With this mental picture, you can stay motivated. Without it, it may feel like the hard work isn't worth it. Don't get confused between enjoying the journey and enjoying the fruits of your labor. You may never enjoy every part of the journey, but it's still worth it if you want to reach your goal. Vision boards, creating a picture, or writing out your Completion story are all ways you can keep your big picture easily accessible.
- The right Mindset will help you reframe negative feelings and keep your enthusiasm up as you push through the more difficult moments. A weak mental Mindset will make it more likely for you to get distracted or shift focus. That's when you pull out your why and remind yourself of the main reason to go through this.

    ➢ *Stick to the plan until I reach my goal.*
    ➢ *Reflect along the way and see the progress I am making.*
    ➢ *Remind myself every day why this is important and who I am doing this for.*

- An accountability partner can be really helpful. Someone to talk to if you're not making progress and to celebrate with you when you are.
- Be proactive about the challenges that could interfere with your progress. Identify and plan for them. Accept the inevitable obstacle and be prepared. Keep handy your YES/NO chart from Step 6.
- Prioritize your time.

Knowing how to use your time wisely is not something people know from birth. Did you either learn it and embrace it, or has it been forced upon you and you fight it? Think back to when you were a child and were supposed to get ready for school in the morning or do your homework after school. Did you grow up with bribery, punishment, nagging, or calm role modeling? Did you naturally do what needed to be done and create your own structure?

Many children learn to do what they have to do (like get dressed) before they are allowed to do what they want to do (play or watch TV). These kids will eventually grow up and discover their autonomy. Their Rebel might think, *the heck with the rules, I'm going to do what I want right now!* Some kids are lucky and learn to use their time wisely; either because their parents are great role models or because they were born with an internal gift of conscientiousness and accountability. Somehow that genetic gift skipped over me—I have to really work at it.

Now that we are adults, it's not as black and white as homework versus play. Maybe it is Project X versus Project Y versus exercise. Maybe our Indulger is stomping its foot and thinking, *I don't want to!* As Les Brown said, "Do what you need to do so that you can do what you want to do" (Brown, 2016).

The truth is, if you want a life of ease and flow, it's time to make peace with your battling inner parts. Have a good long look at what you truly want and what it will take to get there. Then create strategies that will help you stay on course. In doing so, you'll circle back around to commitment, that elusive feeling that wanders off or gets distracted and finds a new goal to cherish.

Conscious prioritization leads to continued commitment.

Exercise 45: Prioritize

1. What does prioritizing your time look like?
2. What do you want to prioritize?
3. What would that look like in your daily, weekly, and/or monthly schedule?
4. What are you committing to?
5. What tools will you use to help you? An app? A whiteboard? A calendar?

THE EXHILARATION OF COMPLETION!

Exhilaration, pride, and happiness are just a few of the positive feelings we get when we've completed a really tough project. You might even feel them after you take each big step. I felt that last summer when I completed my big office transformation.

The Back Story

As you know by now, my husband and I live in a very old house built in 1795. The home has been updated many times over the years, including seven years ago when we built an addition. I needed a designated office, but keeping the resale value in mind, we made sure it could also be a large dining room or family room. The addition included a gas fireplace and a large bay window overlooking our beautiful backyard.

The First Decision

Four years ago, when we were expecting over twenty-five people for Thanksgiving dinner, I decided to give up my spacious new office to make it the dining room—permanently. The much smaller old dining room, complete with an antique chandelier, was now my office. We rushed to swap furniture, making sure to have a wonderful dining space for our large family, but in our haste, my office was never properly set up in the new smaller space.

I hated going into that room; it was such a mess. I usually worked in the kitchen or from the dining room table. My office became a dumping ground, like the infamous closet that you throw things into and hope the door stays shut. The only problem was that my husband had to walk through my office to get to his favorite room in the house, the parlor. I felt very guilty on a regular basis, and even more so when COVID-19 hit and he had to work from home.

The Second Decision

By this point I was claiming two rooms: one for all my stuff (the old dining room) and the new dining room (a nicer setting for all my Zoom meetings). It took about a year, but I finally decided to unpack, purge, organize, and move into my real office. I knew it was going to push every button I had (I hate to purge!), yet I was absolutely committed to transforming this charming room into my forever office. My determination had become a *Commitment at any cost* Mindset. I knew it would take me a while, but I was determined to do it right.

I made slow but steady progress for about four months, taking the time to read, sort, and reorganize thirteen years' worth of papers that had never really found a good home. Every box I unpacked and binder I created was worthy of a small celebration. As I completed each hurdle, including recruiting and helping my husband build shelves and a side table, I'd get a little kick of excitement and pride.

The why behind my office reorganization was to feel proud of my surroundings and to set it up in a way that I could easily find anything I needed with just a quick glance or opening of a file. *A place for everything and everything in its place*. It was a proud moment when I had a clean desk, organized binders on shelves, and access to the files I use all the time.

It's a few years later and I'm still using my office full time. It's far from perfect, and God knows I'm not great at maintaining. I'm still working on that part. I'm most organized when I ask myself, *What do I need to keep, and where should I put it that gives me the best access to the most important items?* Upon Reflection, it's time to set a new goal of keeping my office tidy every day. It's time to start a new Action Cycle.

Completion Step Tips

The first thing I want to remind you is that it's never too late to revisit and complete something you started, even if it's several years old. Prioritize what you'd like to do first and use the Action Cycle to accomplish the next step.

There are a number of strategies to stay the course all the way to Completion:

- Name your goal and what Completion looks like without hedging. No *Maybe I'll get it this far* thoughts. Decide now what counts as "Yes, I did it" or "No, I didn't complete it."
- Remember your why.
- Write a Completion story and immortalize it as a picture, vision board, or chart.
- Keep an empowered Mindset.
- Find an accountability partner.
- Be proactive by Planning for inevitable obstacles.
- Prioritize your time.
- Celebrate all the small wins with fun ways to reward yourself.
- Plan to maintain your strategy if maintenance applies to this goal.

Exercise 46: Write Your Completion Story

Write a Completion story as if your desired outcome has already happened. Include why this was important, what hypothetical steps you took, how you feel now, and how your life has changed. What did you use as your mental picture or vision board? What was your Mindset throughout the project, and what helped you prioritize your time? If you really want to stay successful, include steps that will help you maintain your accomplishments.

STEP 8
REFLECTION

> *We do not learn from experience.*
> *We learn from reflecting on experience.*
>
> —John Dewey

- ➤ Celebration, Evaluation, and Next Steps
- ➤ Personal Growth
- ➤ Lessons Learned
- ➤ Post-Project Reflections

 The task or project is done. You're relieved and happy, and now it's time for **Reflection** so that you can move forward. Reflection is a valuable process for growing, maintaining, and improving ourselves and our strategies, preventing future issues, and stopping us from reinventing the wheel. By taking the time for Reflection, you can not only save time on the next task or project but be able to absorb or synthesize what you've learned.

The bigger the accomplishment and the more skills and habits you develop, the more valuable the Reflection. Even if you failed miserably—especially if you failed miserably—spending time on Reflection can be critical to your ability to keep moving forward. When I think of Reflection, I think of celebration, evaluation, and next steps. I also think about acknowledging my personal growth.

While Reflection is the last step of the Action Cycle, it's important to remember that you can take time to reflect at any point. Evaluating as you go helps you be more aware of your progress and any adjustments you need to make along the way. However, don't forget the most crucial part: the final Reflection after Completion.

CELEBRATION, EVALUATION, AND NEXT STEPS

Celebration comes when you acknowledge that you were able to complete something, step by step and through to the end. You can celebrate small steps you've taken along the way as well as when you reach the end of the Action Cycle. Whether it's a quick, "Yes!," a scoop of your favorite ice cream, or a big post-event party, it's important to take a little time to savor the feeling. Celebrating is another way of adding gas to your engine to keep you motivated. We humans tend to focus on the negative, what went wrong, and how we failed. We need to retrain our minds to look for the good. Celebrating our wins is one way to do that, which is why it's always the first step in my coaching sessions.

There are many methods of evaluation. For your own project review, you might journal or discuss with a trusted friend, peer, or coach. Use questions to evaluate all aspects of the project and the plans for maintaining them:

1. What went well?
2. What would you do again?
3. Were there any challenges along the way? How did you handle them?
4. What might you do differently next time?
5. How will you prepare for the next big project?

If you've completed a team project, I recommend having a formal group meeting with a Reflection agenda. I found several references to an "After-Action Review," a tool that's often used in project management to compare intended results with actual outcomes. Regardless of the user, the tool tends to focus on four key questions as a launching point:

1. What was expected to happen?
2. What actually occurred?
3. What went well and why?
4. What can be improved and how?

Evaluation of Recurring Events and Projects

You don't want to reinvent the wheel each time you approach a recurring project or event. If you finish something you're likely to do again, you can plan ahead to make it easier the next time. That way, each and every time you start off ahead of the game with a plan going into it that can be altered and adjusted as needed. What events or tasks happen on a regular basis in your life, both personally and professionally? How might Reflection make the process easier for you? Consider the following examples:

- ❖ Gardening: prepare for each season ahead of time by stocking up on supplies and making lists of regular tasks that need to be completed at certain intervals.
- ❖ Holidays: delegate meal prep, decorating, and other tasks to the same family members each year.
- ❖ Travel: make a digital packing list (perhaps one for each season) that you can refer to for every trip, as well as a checklist of details to confirm such as hotel and flight reservations.
- ❖ Business Processes: set aside time for a review at the end of every year, walking through wins, challenges, and what you want to do more of or let go of, then flow right into brainstorming for next year's goals; look for my End of Year Review Worksheet at MonicaLeggett.com.

Next Steps

What comes next? You've organized, created a system, made a big decision about a big life transition, and/or completed your training in some new skill or process. You've reached a goal. What will you do next? To pick the next Action steps, start the Action Cycle all over again with new Awareness, Acceptance, and an improved agility to focus your Mindset on what you want. You're prepared to ease right in!

There may be an obvious next step. If the goal you completed requires maintenance, then you know what to focus on next. How will you maintain the growth that you've achieved (the new health, organization, or business success, for instance)? New changes can disappear if we don't reinforce them. That's why it's important to make a maintenance plan for supporting those changes and keeping them going. Don't wait, or all that you've accomplished could be lost. Maintenance may differ depending on your completed task, goal, or project, but there's probably some new routine or system that will keep you on track. Make that your new goal.

If you're coming up blank, with no new goal in mind, continue the Reflection as a bridge to a new Action Cycle. Reflect on what you've learned and explore new ideas, beginning with Awareness.

Personal Growth

What are the long-term effects of all this proactive and mindful work? They surely include deepening new habits, maintaining new systems, remembering how to set a decisive and positive Mindset rather than staying stuck, and taking Action consistently. You've become a new version of yourself, with new Awareness, commitment, and skills that allow you to take on the next goals, habits, and challenges with that much more ease. Acknowledge the work it took to take new Action steps to achieve your success. Be proud of who you've become and the journey you're still on. The more you grow in all areas of your life, the more satisfied and less stressed you'll be.

Personal growth is reflected in how much your doubt or internal conflict has subsided, just as much if not more than looking at what you've accomplished. Are you better able to live your life authentically, consistently, and without the struggle and angst you had at the start of this journey? Remember, it's about *progress, not perfection.*

Exercise 47: Reflect on Your Personal Growth

Ask yourself the following questions.:

1. How have I changed in the course of solving this problem or achieving this goal?
2. What characteristics or traits did I develop?
3. What new habits are forming, and how can I maintain them?
4. What old habits are waning?

Ongoing Self-Reflection Leads to the Next Goal

Part of personal growth is being able to see some gaps we never realized we had. For instance, an emerging leader in a small company is shy, lacks confidence, and doubts themself. They notice after completing some projects with their team that they could be doing a better job managing the team and the way they work on projects together. The emerging leader wants to feel more confident.

Rather than avoiding the issue, the leader can take a course, read some books, turn to someone for assistance (a coach perhaps), and/or ask themself the following questions to begin the Awareness step of the Action Cycle:

1. *What do I want?*
2. *What am I doing well? When do I feel most confident?*
3. *What are the biggest challenges that make me doubt myself?*
4. *Are those doubtful thoughts really true?*
5. *What will I do about them?*

6. *What skills, activities, or support would help me to grow my confidence?*

LESSONS LEARNED

What lessons have you learned—possibly the hard way? Here are a few of mine:

- ❖ If you ignore a medical issue, it can get worse!
- ❖ If you set your mind to do something and have a plan, it's easier to work at it each day.
- ❖ You always want to stay at least one step ahead of kids! (See the upcoming story.)
- ❖ Break down big projects into smaller steps.
- ❖ When trying to do two big things at once, consider how they might be fighting against each other. Take the time to see the big picture for how to work on two things at once.
- ❖ Believe in myself.

Time management strategies are an acquired skill and helpful for any circumstance.

Young children, especially ones with limited attention spans, need a special approach to get them to do things and manage their time well. You might think you have plenty of time to get them into the car to take them somewhere, but those minutes get eaten up by a mysterious time warp. Suddenly, you're late and have to rush. The same can be said about any human, no matter their age or special needs.

> Several years ago, I was babysitting for my grandkids while my daughter Christine and her husband, Morgan, were away on vacation. They live 180 miles from my house, so I don't get to see them as often as I'd like. This was going to be an opportunity to spend some quality time with the grandkids, and I looked forward to being there.
>
> Charlotte was in first grade and my grandson, Stephen, was in preschool. Christine thought it best that they kept their full schedule while I was there. That meant I would have their school hours to do any work I had—coach clients, do some reading or writing—as well as some alone time, which every adult needs.
>
> As Christine reviewed her instruction list with me, she pointed out one of the most important bits of advice that I'll always remember: "Get up fifteen minutes before the kids have to be up so you can stay ahead of them." You would think I would've remembered this from my own days as a young mom, but I didn't understand the power of Acceptance back then.
>
> To explain, I'm not a morning person; neither is my daughter. We love to sleep in, staying in our nice warm covers until we absolutely have to get up, while my husband and Morgan are early birds, up with the sun. Unfortunately, I was going to have a week alone with two children and no built-in

early bird to get the kids ready. I would have to do it all. (Awareness and Acceptance.)

My Mindset for this week was, *Grammie can do this when she stays one step ahead!* I was going to meet this challenge and be the best grammie ever! (An empowered Mindset and positive self-talk are powerful.)

There are so many keys to having a successful and efficient day. The evening prep beforehand is an essential one. I had the kids' bags ready the night before, knew exactly what I was going to prepare for breakfast and lunch, and went to bed earlier than normal. I had a list of what I would do each day while they were in school so that I didn't get distracted by any bright shiny objects. Also, I talked with the kids about what we could do each day to have fun after school. Play games, take a walk, and go to the library were added to our list. (Assessing and Planning).

When the alarm went off each morning, the Current Me would've hit the snooze button for an extra ten minutes, but "Grammie-in-Charge" got out of bed and got dressed right away. Each day, I was up before the kids, we dressed and ate breakfast, and we were out the door at the appointed time. I followed the plan for success. And it worked! (Action—check!)

My Lessons Learned

- ❖ The early bird gets to have a stress-free morning.
- ❖ Prepping the night before makes the morning easier.
- ❖ Positive self-talk is a morale booster and makes for a better experience.

❖ Including the kids in the plans makes it feel like a collaboration.

It's time to use those same lessons learned in my current, non-grandkid days! Imagine how helpful it would be to regularly follow this list:

❖ Prep the night before, make a list of priorities, and create a plan.
❖ Get up fifteen minutes earlier.
❖ Keep up the positive self-talk.

Reflection helps us maintain or repeat any system we've put into place, assess and acknowledge what we've learned, and then apply it to the same issue or a new issue in the future. In the process, we'll change in some way, learn something new, or start a new habit or routine. Reflecting on our progress gives us the inspiration to tackle the next big thing on our to-do lists and leads us to our next goal. It may include your health, business, neglected friendships, or a passion project. Perhaps it will be a life-changing decision such as retirement, moving to a new state, or caring for your elderly parents. You've tackled big things in the past, and you can tackle the next big thing as well.

POST-PROJECT REFLECTIONS

I realized the value of Reflection after dealing with some of my own personal and professional experiences. You've already heard about my gaining back weight because I didn't reflect on my success or plan my next goal of maintenance. Let me share another story from a post-project point of view.

Melissa, my younger daughter, is an active mom working a part-time job and raising two rambunctious boys with her husband, Chris. Melissa, like me, is a very social person who thrives on connecting with other moms in her community. It's no surprise that she's on a social committee for her HOA. They plan events for the kids, the parents, the families in the community, and sometimes the whole town.

In relation to the Action Cycle, the committee gathers facts and interests (Awareness), decides what they're willing to do (Acceptance), and puts their heads together to explore ideas with a fun and realistic Mindset: *Let's do what we can with the manpower we have and have fun while we're doing it. Don't stress out!* They assess their options, start Planning out the events, and take turns organizing, marketing, and executing them (Action to Completion).

Reflection comes in the form of a post-event committee discussion and evaluation of whether the event was a success. This leads to asking questions such as, "Should we do this again next month, next year, or never?" Without that last step of a group Reflection, it's possible that the committee would continue to have the same events over and over or make abrupt decisions based on one bad experience. Reflection gives them the time and opportunity to celebrate, evaluate, maintain, or explore new options or variations. It also creates the opportunity to share what each person did on the project so there's more shared knowledge for future events. Finally, Reflection allows them to confidently state what they will or won't do next time—if there is a next time.

When the busy summer season was over, they got together as a committee for Reflection, asking questions like these:

- ❖ What went well?
- ❖ What events need tweaking?
- ❖ What should we leave out next year?
- ❖ Is there anything else we might add?
- ❖ What will we commit to for next year, in what month, and who will be in charge?

With that Reflection, they've done the work to ease right into the following year. All that's left to do is execute the plan!

How can you translate that same experience to one you've had? Are there ongoing committees, projects, or sweeping events going on in your life that you do with others? These same questions could be used for a small business or a large corporation. Committee participation is very different from solo work. It's essential to complete the Action Cycle as a group so that you have group input, group Action, group Reflection, and group success. You'll have a lot less stress and drama too.

Reflection for Solo-Preneurs

One of the challenging issues for a solo entrepreneur is the lack of a sounding board to talk out ideas, vent frustrations, and find support when they're struggling to get an idea off the ground. They don't have a committee to ask, delegate to, or reflect with. I've worked with countless entrepreneurs who want to launch a new service, offer a workshop, or develop a new signature presentation, but they struggle to get into

Action. If this is you, finding someone to support you, such as a coach or a mastermind group for business owners, can really help when you want to keep moving forward.

Stories of Reflection

- ❖ Two coaches worked as a team to offer training to business professionals. To draw an audience, they set up several information sessions with different themes at their local chamber of commerce. They also contacted people on their email list to drive interest in the workshop. A limited discussion (Reflection) happened after each of the four information sessions and after the full-day workshop. They used those sessions to decide how to improve their training materials and grow their partnership.

- ❖ A certified coach was working with a particular type of client and was really excited about the work they were doing together. Once the coach found their ideal client, Reflection helped them find similar clients in the future:

    → *What do I enjoy about working with this client?*
    → *What else could it lead to?*
    → *Where did this client come from?*
    → *How might I get more of these types of clients?*

- ❖ A massage therapist has noticed that she's struggling with her landlord and has declining foot traffic to her business. She works alone, feeling lonely and isolated. While reflecting on the issue, she asks herself these questions:

- *What are the pros and cons of staying in this location?*
- *What have I tried so far that is or is not working?*
- *Do I like being totally on my own?*
- *Would I be more comfortable and successful in a group setting, such as a wellness center, that has colleagues and more foot traffic?*

❖ While I was having a group discussion with several coaches about our personal and professional lives, Rhonda shared, "I need to change my thoughts around success, failure, and getting things done—how I define them. I need to adjust my expectations." She's so good at Reflection, introspection, and being an observer of her thoughts that she was already shifting them. Rhonda no longer thinks, *I'll only be happy if I get everything done.* She celebrates by thinking, *Look what I got done!* This has helped put her mind at ease rather than constantly driving her to do and be more. Progress, not perfection! It took Reflection to see the thoughts she had around success and failure, and to shift her thoughts over time.

Redefining Success

As Rhonda did, we can redefine what success is by taking time for Reflection. It's okay to get some and not all tasks on your to-do list completed in a day. Rather than considering yourself a failure, consider it an opportunity to celebrate while realizing that prioritizing and staying focused shortened the list!

Successful thoughts: *Today was a great day. I did most of what I needed to do and made some time for myself and my husband. I'll finish as much as I can tomorrow.*

Unsuccessful thoughts: *Ugh. I didn't get everything done, and I took a break when I really didn't have time.*

Defining success is different for every person you ask. Even when you first begin a journey to success, things can happen that will adjust your final destination. What you thought was part of success could suddenly become unimportant. The trick to finding success is knowing that it's all relative! Are you feeling successful at this moment with this thought, task, or result? If not, what will you do about it?

Success comes with Reflection and adjustment. Can you be present every day in your life and accept feeling successful now rather than when life is perfect? Guess what—life will never be perfect! Be happy with what now is bringing you, and success will follow. Success isn't really the destination that everyone imagines it to be. Just like happiness, you don't have to wait to feel it. Choose to feel it now. Count every blessing as a success.

Exercise 48: Reflect on the Process

1. What was expected to happen and what actually occurred?
2. What went well, and what could be better?
3. How can I improve those things?
4. What system, routine, or habit did I put into place?

5. What is my new identity, and what new skill(s) did I utilize?
6. What challenges did I overcome?
7. What energized me or drained me in the process?
8. What things do I want to maintain, and how will I maintain them?
9. What comes next?
10. Is there something obvious that will continue from this completed goal?

You've read about the eight steps and begun to put them into Action. What are you more aware of now? Is there anything you've accomplished that felt easier and helped you leave the struggle behind? What steps in the cycle are you excelling at, and which are giving you a bit of trouble? The answers to your questions will deepen your Awareness and give you the space to be more intentional next time.

If you're struggling or getting stuck, don't lose heart. Practice is the key to accelerated growth. The better you get at overcoming daily challenges, the better you'll be at conquering big life transitions, overwhelming decisions, and scary conversations. Try breaking down your larger steps into even smaller, more manageable, and realistic goals.

You can download a PDF of the Action Cycle at MonicaLeggett.com.

CONCLUSION

My original goal in writing this book was to not only help you go from doubtful to decisive and take Action for one situation but also provide you with new strategies to use throughout your life. Over time, I realized I wanted more out of this book. I wanted to help you get to the finish line with consistency and evaluate what worked and didn't work so that you can control your life's trajectory.

We have a paradoxical challenge before us: to accept rather than judge ourselves for who we are *and* to set our sights on new skills, strengths, and characteristics that will influence our actions. A parallel paradox is the concept of setting goals yet never arriving at our final destination. Our lives are a series of desired outcomes and goals. If we accept that life is a never-ending journey and celebrate our wins along the way, we'll never be dissatisfied. Satisfaction comes from knowing we made something happen. We made a decision, took Action, and saw results.

You are no longer the same person who picked up this book. You've learned the value of making shifts, understanding yourself, and proactively working your way through the Action Cycle. At any given moment, you have the potential to become your Best Self and live your Best Life—whatever that means to you.

Let's reflect on what I hope this particular journey has taught you:

- ❖ **It takes a shift to see new results**—a shift in your focus, your intentions, and your level of commitment. To become decisive, you have to be all in and know what you want and why. No more "maybe" and "someday." Proactively addressing rather than ignoring or avoiding life's challenges allows you to explore new paths. The biggest shifts are those in your thoughts and your actions. When your thoughts change, your actions change, and then your life changes.

- ❖ **Investing time to understand yourself will reap great rewards.** This involves exploring your nature and the way you were nurtured, including all the experiences that led to your current beliefs and values. Your inner parts influence your thoughts, your ability to be decisive, your priorities, and your goals. Reframing to a more empowered Mindset will change your whole approach to life. All change begins with Awareness, and the most helpful place to begin is with yourself.

- ❖ **The Action Cycle is your guide to achieving the results you want.** I purposefully left the steps of the cycle for the end of this book because I wanted to first lay the foundation of what could make the eight steps go more smoothly. Everything you learned in Parts 1 and 2 of this book was an exercise in Awareness—Step 1 of the Action Cycle. Awareness begins with understanding what you want and who you are at the core, then exploring ways to make the many shifts I've proposed. Identifying your desired outcomes, accepting and owning change, reframing your thoughts, identifying and dealing with challenges and inner parts, Assessing options, creating plans, setting intentions with commitment and decisiveness, and taking Action all the way to Completion and Reflection is the path from doubtful to decisive.

❖ **Living your Best Life with decisiveness, focus, and direction takes work, but it's worth it!** With these tools, strategies, and new intentions, you're bound to enjoy the journey.

I invite you to join our community to find support and learn from one another. I look forward to knowing how you're applying everything you've learned and about the goals you're achieving. Reach out to me at MonicaLeggett.com.

GLOSSARY

There may be a few acronyms, words, and phrases I use throughout the book that may be new to you. Some of them are my own creation or interpretation, some I've credited to people and organizations I admire, and others I've taken from the dictionary.

Achilles heel: a small problem or weakness in a person or system that can result in failure

The Action Cycle: an eight-step process to help you overcome obstacles, take action, and see new results.

1. **Awareness**: having insight of what is working, what is not, and what you want; a pattern you notice about yourself, others, or a situation
2. **Acceptance**: acknowledgment of reality and situations; taking ownership for change
3. **Mindset**: the way you perceive your world and the lens through which you view your options; perspective; attitude
4. **Assessing**: weighing the options available to resolve your challenge; exploring possibilities
5. **Planning**: deciding the who, what, where, and when for your actions with the best options available
6. **Action**: taking steps toward your goal, including Planning, creating systems, and tracking your progress

7. **Completion**: completing all the steps to achieve a desired outcome
8. **Reflection**: noticing where you have come from and where you ended up; celebrating your growth and learning from your experiences

ADD Approach: deciding whether you will address an issue yourself, delegate it to someone else, or dismiss it

Affirmations: "statements that we say to ourselves that can shift our mindset and make us feel better about ourselves" (Davis 2021)

Best Life: living what you truly want for all aspects of your life

Best Self: the clear-minded version of the Self who is free of limiting thoughts brought on by inner parts

Big Hairy Audacious Goal (BHAG): a compelling goal that can both inspire and scare you at the same time

Blended: "when the feelings and beliefs of one part merge with another part or the Self" (Schwartz 2023, 151).

Coaching: "the process of partnering with clients in a thought-provoking and creative process that inspires them to maximize their personal and professional potential" (International Coaching Federation n.d.)

COAL: an acronym meaning an attitude of being curious, open, accepting, and loving toward yourself (Fogel 2014).

Current Me: who I am in the present moment

Easing In: working your way into a larger goal by taking smaller, gradual steps

Expected Value: the anticipated benefit of an investment at some point in the future

Flow: when life proceeds smoothly and readily

Gaming your plan: a way to increase your chances of reaching your goal by adding fun, creative, or proactive steps to your plan that help you overcome your typical obstacles

Habits: behaviors that automatically follow a cue or trigger

Habit stacking: when you add one new habit to a habit that already exists (Scott 2017)

High switching costs: the cost to your bottom line of focus, energy, and productivity while switching between different tasks

Holistic approach: looking at a complete system rather than at individual parts

Inner parts: unique subpersonalities of the mind, as described by Internal Family Systems

Internal Family Systems: "a transformative tool that conceives every human being as a system of protective and wounded inner parts lead by a core Self" (Internal Family Systems Institute n.d.b.)

The Judge: "master Saboteur, the one everyone suffers from" causing you "to find faults with yourself, others, and your conditions and circumstances"; "generates much of your anxiety, stress, anger, disappointment, shame, and guilt"; the Judge has nine **Accomplice Saboteurs** (Chamine 2012):

1. **Avoider / Procrastinator**: finds reasons to delay action and avoid conflict; "focuses on the pleasant and positive in extreme ways"
2. **Controller**: "anxiety-based need to take charge and control situations and people's actions to one's own will; high anxiety and impatience when that is not possible"

3. **Hyper-Achiever**: "dependent on constant performance and achievement for self-respect and self-validation; latest achievement quickly discounted, needing more"
4. **Hyper-Rational**: "intense and exclusive focus on the rational processing of everything, including relationships" and "limits your depth and flexibility in relationships"
5. **Hyper-Vigilant**: "makes you feel intense and continuous anxiety about all the dangers surrounding you and what could go wrong"
6. **Pleaser**: "indirectly tries to gain acceptance and affection by helping, pleasing, rescuing, or flattering others"; "loses sight of own needs and becomes resentful as a result"
7. **Restless**: "constantly in search of greater excitement in the next activity or through perpetual busyness; rarely at peace or content with the current activity"
8. **Stickler**: takes "the need for perfection, order, and organization too far," which makes "you and others around you anxious and uptight"; becomes "anxious trying to make too many things perfect"
9. **Victim**: acts "emotional and temperamental as a way to gain attention and affection"; has "an extreme focus on internal feelings, particularly painful ones"; "martyr streak"

Judge-O-Meter: a tool to discern whether an action, thought, or situation has a positive or negative effect

Limiting beliefs: thoughts about yourself or others that limits the belief in your ability to move forward or accomplish a task

MAP: acronym for Mindset, Assessment, and Plan

Glossary

Mind map: a visual representation of ideas, tasks, or processes that allows you to capture your thoughts as you brainstorm solutions in a structured manner

Mindfulness: "Mindfulness is the basic human ability to be fully present, aware of where we are and what we're doing, and not overly reactive or overwhelmed by what's going on around us" (Mindful.org, n.d.).

Mindset: the way you perceive your world and the lens through which you view your options; perspective; attitude

Model: to demonstrate a particular behavior or skill

Neural pathways: a series of connected nerves along which electrical impulses travel in the body

Outcome Statement: a declaration of what you want to create at a high level that also explains why this is important to you

PeopleMap™ System: a system of assessment tools, co-created by E. Michael Lillibridge, PhD and licensed psychologist, to improve communication within couples and teams; the basic assessment determines your level of each of the following four personality types: Leader, People, Task, and Free Spirit. For a full description of each type, please visit their website at https://www.peoplemapsystems.com/personality-types/; Monica Leggett is a certified trainer of the PeopleMap System

Perspective Wheel: a coaching tool to help identify multiple perspectives as options that may enable you to approach an issue or challenge a new way; for example, instead of seeing it as *This is impossible,* you might try the *Give it a try* or *What is one thing I can do?* perspective.

Positive Intelligence Quotient (PQ): "the percentage of time your mind is acting as your friend rather than your enemy" (Chamine 2012, 7)

Positive Intelligence Assessment: quickly determines the intensity of your Saboteurs; available free online at https://www.positiveintelligence.com/. Monica Leggett is a Positive Intelligence Coach and guides people through an eight-week program based on this work.

RAFT: a process of using your desired results, actions, feelings, and thoughts to achieve your desired outcomes

Reframing: adjusting your thoughts to a new way of looking at things; looking at something with a new perspective

Return on investment: what you gain in either money, results, or anything else of value from an investment you make of your time, money, or energy

Saboteur: an inner part that sabotages your desired actions and outcomes by manipulating your thoughts

Sage: "the deeper and wiser part of you" (what I call our Best Self); it can "resist getting carried away by the drama and tension of the moment or falling victim to the lies of the Saboteurs" (Chamine 2012, 20)

Self: an essence at the core of our thinking that is influenced by the many inner parts the mind has created either as protection or as a result of trauma (Internal Family Systems Institute, n.d.a.)

Survivor Brain: "the part of the brain tasked with helping us survive"; consists of the most primitive parts of the brain, the brain stem, and the limbic system and is involved in initiating our response to danger; the left brain is the primary hemisphere involved in the survival focus, "with its concentration on concrete data and detail" (Chamine 2012, 211)

SMART goals: goals that are specific, measurable, attainable, realistic, and timely (a specific time frame to complete the goal); the R may also include resonant (meaningful to you) and the T thrilling

Transtheoretical Model / Stages of Change Model: a model developed by James Prochaska and Carlo DiClemente in the late 1970s that describes the six stages a person goes through with behavioral change: precontemplation, contemplation, preparation, action, maintenance, and termination; first used to describe people attempting to or successfully quit smoking

Treetop Planner: a brainstorming or organizational tool to write down all the upcoming tasks or desired steps to take, placed into specific boxes according to projects or areas of your life; more functional than a to-do list in that steps are categorized to help prioritize

Unblended: "the state of being-with in which no part (e.g. feeling, thought sensation, belief) is overwhelming the Self" (Anderson, Sweezy, and Schwartz 2017, 5)

Yes/No Exercise: a coaching tool to list what you will say yes to and no to in order to set boundaries and assist goal achievement, such as "I will say no to sweets"

REFERENCES

Anderson, Frank G., Martha Sweezy, and Richard C. Schwartz. 2017. *Internal Family Systems Skills Training Manual: Trauma-Informed Treatment for Anxiety, Depression, PTSD & Substance Abuse*. Eau Claire, WI: PESI Publishing and Media.

Brookes, Elisabeth. n.d. "Transtheoretical Model: Stages of Health Behavior Change." SimplyPsychology. Last modified April 13, 2023. https://www.simplypsychology.org/transtheoretical-model.html.

Brown, Les. 2016. "Do what you need to do, so that you can do what you want to do." Facebook, June 3, 2026. https://www.facebook.com/thelesbrown/posts/do-what-you-need-to-do-so-that-you-can-do-what-you-want-to-do-success-and-conven/10154169658299654/.

Center for The Empowerment Dynamic. n.d.a. "The Karpman Drama Triangle: How to Avoid Falling into It!" Accessed July 23, 2023. https://theempowermentdynamic.com/karpman-drama-triangle/.

Center for The Empowerment Dynamic. n.d.b. "The Secret to How People Change." Accessed July 20, 2023. https://theempowermentdynamic.com/the-secret-to-how-people-change-2/.

Chamine, Shirzad. 2012. *Positive Intelligence: Why Only 20% of Teams and Individuals Achieve Their True Potential and*

How You Can Achieve Yours. Austin, TX: Greenleaf Book Group Press.

Collins, Jim, and Jerry I. Porras. 2004. *Built to Last: Successful Habits of Visionary Companies*. New York: HarperCollins.

Covey, Stephen. 1989. *7 Habits of Highly Effective People*. New York: Simon & Schuster.

Davis, Tchiki. 2021. "A Guide to Affirmations and How to Use Them." *Psychology Today*. https://www.psychologytoday.com/us/blog/click-here-happiness/202105/guide-affirmations-and-how-use-them.

Duckworth, Angela. 2018. *Grit: The Power of Passion and Perseverance*. New York: Scribner.

Emerald, David. 2010. *The Power of TED* (*The Empowerment Dynamic)*, 2nd ed. Bainbridge Island, WA: Polaris Publishing.

Ethics Unwrapped. n.d. "Values." Accessed July 21, 2023. https://ethicsunwrapped.utexas.edu/glossary/values.

Fogel, Steven J. 2014. "Mindful Awareness and COAL." August 25, 2014. https://stevenjayfogel.com/mindful-awareness-and-coal/.

Friedman, Gillian, and Emma Goldberg. 2022. "The Pandemic Wrecked Millions of Careers. These 6 People Built New Ones." *New York Times*, March 26, 2022.

Goodman, Brenda. 2016. "Research Sheds Light on Why People Who Lose Weight Gain It Back." MedicineNet, October 14, 2023. https://www.medicinenet.com/script/main/art.asp?articlekey=198749.

International Coaching Federation. n.d. "All Things Coaching." Accessed July 28, 2023. https://coachingfederation.org/about.

Internal Family Systems Institute. n.d.a. "Evolution of The Internal Family Systems Model by Dr. Richard Schwartz, Ph.D." Accessed July 24, 2023. https://ifs-institute.com/resources/articles/evolution-internal-family-systems-model-dr-richard-schwartz-ph-d.

Internal Family Systems Institute. n.d.b. "What Is Internal Family Systems?" Accessed July 28, 2023. https://ifs-institute.com.

Kelland, Mark D. (n.d.). "Paul Costa and Robert McCrae and the Five-Factor Model of Personality." LibreTexts | Social Sciences, accessed August 25, 2023. https://socialsci.libretexts.org/Bookshelves/Psychology/Culture_and_Community/Personality_Theory_in_a_Cultural_Context_(Kelland)/10%3A_Trait_Theories_of_Personality/10.07%3A_Paul_Costa_and_Robert_McCrae_and_the_Five-Factor_Model_of_Personality.

Kourlas, Gia. 2022. "What Is the Power of Unity Phelan's Dancing? 'I'm Clay.'" *New York Times*, October 14, 2022.

Lamott, Anne. 1994. *Bird by Bird: Some Instructions on Writing and Life*. New York: Anchor Books.

Larsen, Linda. 2001. *12 Secrets to High Self-Esteem*. Mission, KS: SkillPath.

Leonhardt, Justine. 2022. "What Is the Difference Between Feelings and Emotions?" ThinkPsych, April 21, 2022. https://thinkpsych.com/blog/what-is-the-difference-between-feelings-and-emotions/.

Lillibridge, E. Michael. 1998. *The People Map: Understanding Yourself and Others*. Lutz, FL: Lilmat Press.

Martinez, Eddy. 2022. "TV Personality, Chainsaw Sculpture Wows Derby Middle Schoolers." *Connecticut Post*, October 18, 2022.

Mateos-Aparicio, Pedro, and Antonio Rodriguez-Moreno. 2019. "The Impact of Studying Brain Plasticity." *Frontiers in Cellular Neuroscience* 13, no 66: 1–5. https://doi.org/10.3389/fncel.2019.00066.

Mayo Clinic. n.d. "Cognitive Behavioral Therapy." Accessed July 22, 2023. https://www.mayoclinic.org/tests-procedures/cognitive-behavioral-therapy/about/pac-20384610.

Mindful.org. n.d. "Getting Started with Mindfulness." Accessed April 4, 2023. https://www.mindful.org/meditation/mindfulness-getting-started/.

Scott, S. J. 2017. *Habit Stacking: 127 Small Changes to Improve Your Health, Wealth, and Happiness*. New Jersey: Oldtown Publishing.

Schwartz, Richard C. 2023. *Introduction to Internal Family Systems*. Boulder, CO: Sounds True Inc.

Sounds True. 2023. "All Parts Welcome - Richard Schwartz, PhD + Elizabeth Gilbert: Creativity & Internal Family Systems." YouTube, May 22, 2023, 16:03. https://www.youtube.com/watch?v=VBYrJOK4Dtk.

Thompson, Susan P. 2017. *Bright Line Eating: The Science of Living Happy, Thin, and Free*. Carlsbad, CA: Hay House.

Urban, Tim. 2016. "Inside the Mind of a Master Procrastinator." Filmed February 16, 2016, in Vancouver, Canada. TEDEd, video, 14:04. https://ed.ted.com/lessons/inside-the-mind-of-a-master-procrastinator-tim-urban.

Vaish, Amrisha, Tobias Grossmann, and Amanda Woodward. 2008. "Not All Emotions Are Created Equal: The

Negativity Bias in Social-Emotional Development," *Psychological Bulletin*, 134, no. 1: 383–403. https://doi.org/10.1037/0033-2909.134.3.383.

Zajonc, Donna. 2020. *Who Do You Want to Be on the Way to What You Want?* Bainbridge Island, WA: Polaris.

ABOUT THE AUTHOR

Monica Leggett is an accomplished coach, speaker, and goal accelerator with a passion for helping people make meaningful changes in their personal and professional lives. As a result of her coaching process, Monica's clients learn to build and maintain confidence, clarity, mental fitness, and sustainable habits that empower their lives and relationships—moving forward with new focus and direction.

With certifications and training in a number of coaching programs and tools, Monica has a keen understanding of human behavior and has helped countless individuals and teams unlock their potential and achieve their objectives. Monica is also known to be a "conversation whisperer," helping her clients have crucial conversations that will help them build or mend relationships. Her coaching typically focuses on the intersection of personal and professional development where leadership, communication, self-actualization, and relationship-building reside.

Throughout her career, Monica has worked with a diverse range of clients, including executives, entrepreneurs, educators, managers, couples, and work teams. Monica's coaching style is highly personalized and tailored to the specific needs and goals of each client. Whether working with individuals seeking to improve their leadership skills, entrepreneurs looking to grow their businesses, or teams striving to enhance their performance, Monica uses a holistic approach to help clients achieve their desired outcomes.

Doubtful to Decisive is a legacy project, drawing on over fifteen years of Monica's coaching experience, capturing the concepts, strategies, tools, tips, and exercises of her work. Monica learned long ago that all growth and change begins with Awareness, and that is what coaching and this book are all about.

You can find Monica in her free time crocheting, assembling puzzles, or entertaining family and friends with her husband, Steve, in their antique farmhouse in Connecticut.

CALL TO ACTION

> *Tell me and I forget. Teach me and I remember. Involve me and I learn.*
>
> —Benjamin Franklin

Reading a book can give you great ideas, but absorbing the material, doing the exercises, and making changes in your life can take time.

Go to Monica Leggett.com and increase your personal and professional growth:

- ❖ Sign up for the monthly newsletter for a deeper dive
- ❖ Join Monica in monthly webinars and discussions
- ❖ Host a Book Club Discussion Circle and invite Monica to join you*
- ❖ Become a member of Monica's Membership Circle to access recorded webinars and more
- ❖ Join a Mastermind Group
- ❖ Hire Monica for one-on-one coaching

Experiential learning has helped me become the coach and author I am today. That's why I am creating a community to support the readers of this book. It's easy for fear and old habits to pull you back into the old way of doing things. You can choose to stay on the periphery and read newsletters, or you can join me in webinars, group coaching, or even one-on-one coaching. I also offer a membership with a number of perks, which you can learn about at MonicaLeggett.com. Come join the circle!

One of my greatest hopes is that book clubs will read *Doubtful to Decisive* and create a movement where empowered readers will take back control of their lives and set intentions to create their Best Life and live as their Best Self. There will be circles of friends and associates who discuss, explore, and support each other from their most authentic and honest place. *I will be happy to join at least one group per month in a virtual conversation and connect with readers in person when I can.

If you are curious about Peoplemap(™) or your saboteurs from the Positive Intelligence program, reach out to us at MonicaLeggett.com for more information.

Please keep in touch and share your greatest wins, deepest learning, and favorite outcomes of this work. Let me know of any struggles as well. I know it's not all sunshine and daisies out there, and that's why it's helpful to be in a community.

When I learn something new, the first thing I want to do is share it with others. I hope you'll do the same.

Monica

Contact Monica:
www.MonicaLeggett.com
facebook.com/MonicaLeggettCoachingConsulting
instagram.com/new_steps_life_coaching
linkedin.com/in/monicaleggett
Email: Info@MonicaLeggett.com

BOOK CLUB QUESTIONS

1. What are three circumstances in your "Before" picture that you want to let go of in your "After" picture? In other words, what issues, challenges, tendencies, or decisions do you want to resolve?
2. The author mentions many shifts in Part 1 of the book. How well do you function when you focus on the problem or blame others instead of focusing on the outcome you want?

    a. What helps you stay focused on the outcome?
    b. What other shifts can you relate to or see the value of?

3. In "The Road Less Traveled", the author paints a picture of an overwhelming situation where everything seems to go wrong. When have you ever felt that way and how did you resolve it? How has the metaphor helped you since reading that passage?
4. What is most important for you to move forward; commitment, decisiveness, or confidence? Why? Can you achieve all three? How?
5. In Part 2, what is the connection between Nature, Nurture, and Mindfulness?
6. How do your thoughts affect your results?

    a. What thoughts cause you to feel stuck?
    b. What thoughts help you to move forward and see positive results?

7. What new trails or neuropathways are you working on and for what purpose?
8. What limiting beliefs have you noticed more since reading the book? For example, "I don't have time" or "I'll never accomplish this!" What are you doing now when you notice the limiting thought?
9. What do you know about yourself now that you didn't know before?

    a. What new inner parts do you know better? For example, Judge, Avoider, or Controller?
    b. What default tendencies have been in your way for a long time? What you are letting go of? (Give examples.)

10. What positive inner parts have you started nurturing to help you show up better in life?
11. What goals are you working on as a result of reading this book?
12. Which steps in the Action Cycle are natural for you, and which do you need to practice more?
13. What have you been able to accomplish that you were stuck on before?

    a. How are things different in your life now?

14. What lessons have you learned that you might apply to future challenges? Perhaps a helpful way to handle a situation or a new system or routine to make things easier?
15. Who are you at your finest and best?

Be sure to go to MonicaLeggett.com to stay informed about new opportunities.

If you are hosting a group to discuss *Doubtful to Decisive*, please register your group for a monthly drawing so that Monica might join you (virtually) at your book club circle.

THE B CORP MOVEMENT

Dear reader,

Thank you for reading this book and joining the Publish Your Purpose community! You are joining a special group of people who aim to make the world a better place.

What's Publish Your Purpose About?

Our mission is to elevate the voices often excluded from traditional publishing. We intentionally seek out authors and storytellers with diverse backgrounds, life experiences, and unique perspectives to publish books that will make an impact in the world.

Beyond our books, we are focused on tangible, action-based change. As a woman- and LGBTQ+-owned company, we are committed to reducing inequality, lowering levels of poverty, creating a healthier environment, building stronger communities, and creating high-quality jobs with dignity and purpose.

As a Certified B Corporation, we use business as a force for good. We join a community of mission-driven companies building a more equitable, inclusive, and sustainable global economy. B Corporations must meet high standards of transparency, social and environmental performance, and accountability as determined by the nonprofit B Lab.

The certification process is rigorous and ongoing (with a recertification requirement every three years).

How Do We Do This?

We intentionally partner with socially and economically disadvantaged businesses that meet our sustainability goals. We embrace and encourage our authors and employee's differences in race, age, color, disability, ethnicity, family or marital status, gender identity or expression, language, national origin, physical and mental ability, political affiliation, religion, sexual orientation, socio-economic status, veteran status, and other characteristics that make them unique.

Community is at the heart of everything we do—from our writing and publishing programs to contributing to social enterprise nonprofits like reSET (www.resetco.org) and our work in founding B Local Connecticut.

We are endlessly grateful to our authors, readers, and local community for being the driving force behind the equitable and sustainable world we are building together.

To connect with us online, or publish with us, visit us at www.publishyourpurpose.com.

Elevating Your Voice,

Jenn T Grace

Jenn T. Grace
Founder, Publish Your Purpose

www.ingramcontent.com/pod-product-compliance
Lightning Source LLC
Chambersburg PA
CBHW040302170426
43194CB00021B/2861